THE
UNCHARTED
PASSAGE

THE UNCHARTED PASSAGE

GIRLS' ADOLESCENCE IN THE DEVELOPING WORLD

BARBARA S. MENSCH
JUDITH BRUCE
MARGARET E. GREENE

 Population Council

The Population Council is an international, nonprofit, nongovernmental institu-
tion that seeks to improve the wellbeing and reproductive health of current and
future generations around the world and to help achieve a humane, equitable,
and sustainable balance between people and resources. The Council conducts
biomedical, social science, and public health research and helps build research
capacities in developing countries. Established in 1952, the Council is governed
by an international board of trustees. Its New York headquarters supports a global network of regional and country offices.

Population Council
One Dag Hammarskjold Plaza
New York, NY 10017 USA

Library of Congress Cataloging-in-Publication Data

Mensch, Barbara S.
    The uncharted passage : girls' adolescence in the developing world
/ Barbara S. Mensch, Judith Bruce, and Margaret E. Greene.
        p.   cm.
    Includes bibliographical references.
    ISBN 0-87834-093-9 (pbk. : alk. paper)
    1. Teenage girls--Developing countries--Social conditions.
2. Teenage girls--Developing countries--Economic conditions.
3. Teenage girls--Health and hygiene--Developing countries.
I. Bruce, Judith. II. Greene, Margaret E. III. Title.
HQ799.D44M46   1998
305.235--dc21   98-40824
                                                                                    CIP

Editor: Judith A.M. Outlaw
Cover and text design: Y. Christina Tse

Printed in the United States of America

To our adolescent children
William and Sarah Mensch Evans, and
Rafaela and Paz de la Huerta y Bruce, and
to all adolescent children.

Contents

List of Tables and Figures

Acknowledgments

This book could not have been completed without the efforts of many people. First, we thank colleagues at the World Bank, in particular Thomas Merrick, Anne Tinker, and Debrewerk Zewdie, for financial and moral support in the research phase of this project. Thanks are also extended to our colleagues at the Population Council, John Bongaarts, George Brown, and Margaret Catley-Carlson, for their encouragement and support over the course of the project.

Special thanks go to those who provided us with data, references, and examples of innovative programs and who unselfishly answered our numerous queries over the last three years. In particular, we acknowledge Richard Anker, Ann Blanc, Caroline Bledsoe, Martha Brady, Terese Caouette, Trevor Croft, Bruce Dick, Annabel Erulkar, Jane Ferguson, Stanley Henshaw, Jane Hughes, Kathleen Kurz, Ann McCauley, Leo Morris, Jennefer Sebstad, and Susheela Singh.

Paul Hewett has been extremely patient and skilled in producing DHS tabulations for this volume and modifying them whenever asked. Kirsten Moore conducted valuable research and documentation of innovative programs for adolescent girls. Carey Meyers and Barry Ravitch have been tremendously helpful in inputting text changes, producing tables, and checking references with nary a complaint. Their high level of administrative support, along with that of Diane Rubino, and long hours of work and dedication to the Council's mission over the last few years are greatly appreciated. Design of the publication reflects the considerable talents of Y. Christina Tse. Robert Heidel was as usual a very efficient copy editor.

We thank Ruth Dixon-Mueller and Constance Nathanson for serving as outside reviewers of this volume prior to publication. Their cogent comments and suggestions resulted in a number of modifications and, we hope, improvements. We would also like to thank several colleagues who read and commented on earlier drafts, including John Bongaarts, Adrienne Germain, Nicole Haberland, Barbara Ibrahim, Carol Kaufman, Cynthia B. Lloyd, and Saroj Pachauri.

We owe an enormous intellectual debt to Sajeda Amin and Cynthia B. Lloyd, whose ground-breaking research on livelihoods and education, respectively, has affected our thinking about the transition to adulthood in the developing world. The numerous references to their work are by no means an accident.

Finally, we are tremendously grateful to the editor of this volume, Judith A. M. Outlaw. Her sensitivity to our underlying message, her attention to detail, her ability to translate ideas into clear prose, and her unflagging energy are greatly appreciated.

Chapter 1

Advancing Our Understanding of Adolescent Girls' Experience

Adolescence is a powerfully formative time of transition to adulthood, roughly concurrent with the second decade of life. What happens between the ages of 10 and 19, whether for good or ill, shapes how girls and boys live out their lives as women and men—not only in the reproductive arena, but in the social and economic realm as well. Yet, despite its impact on human development, adolescence has been sidelined as a research and policy subject in developing countries. As a result, we know little about young people's lives in these societies.

Policy interest in adolescence *has* begun to expand—consider the United Nations Convention on the Rights of the Child, which defined childhood as extending through age 18, and the less appealing but prevalent concern about the security implications of large numbers of unemployed youth.[1] Nevertheless, the center of the adolescent *problematique* remains sexual and reproductive behavior. Demographically founded concerns about adolescent fertility have led to inquiries into young people's rates of sexual activity, unintended pregnancy, and childbearing. Concerns within the health community about the alarming increase in the numbers of HIV-infected youth, particularly females, have spawned research on adolescent sexual behavior and reproductive health. These are important subjects of study, but they have often been dealt with superficially. In particular, gender issues have been greatly neglected in this

---

[1] Because of their large and growing numbers and their disproportionate representation among rural-to-urban migrants (Oucho and Gould 1993), adolescents are perceived as a security risk. Some analysts argue that masses of unemployed, on-the-move youth (i.e., adolescent males) pose a threat to civil society (Kennedy 1993). The Central Intelligence Agency Task Force on State Failure included a "youth bulge variable" (the ratio of 15–24-year-olds to 30–55-year-olds) in their quantitative model predicting political stability. This variable was one of three out of 75 that best predicted a state failure involving communal conflict (Esty et al. 1995).

> **Girls' social and economic disadvantages are the driving forces behind early marriage and childbearing.**

research—despite the fact that many more girls than boys marry and/or have a child before age 20. Moreover, adolescence is precisely when gender role differentiation intensifies.

Girls and boys in cultures throughout the world are treated differently from birth onward (and even antenatally where selective abortion of female fetuses is practiced), but at puberty this gender divide widens (Bruce, Lloyd, and Leonard 1995). During adolescence, the world expands for boys and contracts for girls. Boys enjoy new privileges reserved for men; girls endure new restrictions reserved for women. Boys gain autonomy, mobility, opportunity, and power (including power over girls' sexual and reproductive lives); girls are systematically deprived of these assets.[2]

The English language fosters blindness to, and neglect of, the distinctive experiences of adolescent girls. Paradoxically, just at this stage when gender roles diverge sharply, language homogenizes gender. Males and females are "boys and girls" as children, and "men and women" as adults. In between, gender differences dissolve into androgynous appellatives: adolescent, teenager, young adult, young person. This linguistic lumping together of male and female adolescents masks the inequities of their experience.

Girls' social and economic disadvantages have many direct and indirect effects on their reproductive behavior and health. We argue that these disadvantages are, in fact, the driving forces behind early marriage and childbearing. They largely account for the fact that more than 40 percent of girls in the developing world give birth before the age of 20 (Bos et al. 1994; Singh 1998b).[3]

The world is now populated by the largest generation of youth in human history—and the next generation will be even larger. There are now roughly 900 million 10–19-year-olds in developing countries; by the year 2005, their numbers will exceed 1 billion (Bos et al. 1994).[1] Even if average fertility were to fall rapidly to the replacement rate of 2.1 births per woman, the sheer number of females giving birth over the next decade will be so large that population will continue to grow rapidly for

---

[2] This pattern varies in different geographic settings, socioeconomic groups, and families and, of course, does not apply to every individual.

[3] This statistic masks considerable variation across regions. It is based on surveys of 20–24-year-olds in 43 countries representing 75 percent of the developing-world population outside China. Actual figures are 42 percent for all 43 countries, 55 percent for sub-Saharan Africa, 33 percent for Latin America, and 26 percent for North Africa. The fertility data are drawn from Singh (1998b) and the population data are taken from Bos et al. (1994). Aggregated figures were calculated by computing a weighted average of the percentage of girls giving birth before age 20, such that individual countries contribute to the aggregate in proportion to their population size.

some time. This phenomenon of "population momentum" will account for about half of future population growth in the developing world up to the year 2100 (Bongaarts 1994).[5] Raising the average age at which females begin childbearing—thereby lengthening the span between generations—could yield substantial and closely linked social, economic, and demographic dividends. For example, if the mean age of childbearing[6] in Bangladesh were to rise by five years, approximately 40 percent of population growth attributable to momentum would be averted (Bongaarts 1998) and the wellbeing of young females would almost certainly improve. Because the age at which females begin childbearing is largely determined by the social, economic, and gender dynamics operating in their lives, we should understand these dynamics even if our concerns are strictly demographic.

While all adolescents deserve our attention, the needs of adolescent girls in the developing world are particularly pressing. Furthermore, their wellbeing is crucial to the social cohesiveness and economic productivity of their societies. For these reasons, our monograph focuses on adolescent girls. Their experience during the critical second decade of their lives shapes their future and, by extension, the future of the societies in which they live.

Characterizing adolescence

Adolescence has a relatively short history, both as a recognized stage in the life span of girls, in particular, and as a subject of research. To the extent that anthropologists have studied the transition to adulthood,

---

[4] World Bank figures are 894,216,000 in 1995 and 1,047,558,000 in 2005. Expanding birth cohorts are primarily responsible for this projected increase, but successful child health initiatives in the developing world have also increased the proportion of children surviving into adolescence.

[5] John Bongaarts (1994), who has significantly advanced our understanding of population growth, divides future growth into three components: unwanted fertility, high desired family size (that is, fertility preferences above two children per woman), and population momentum. His decomposition, which assumes that the World Bank projection of future population growth will prove correct, attributes a portion of this projected growth to each of the three components. The World Bank projects that global population will be 10.2 billion in 2100; for this to be the case, there must be substantial declines in unwanted fertility and desired fertility from present levels, and perhaps increases in women's age at first childbearing as well. These demographic changes, which are assumed in the World Bank projection, are not part of Bongaarts's decomposition; thus past and current investments in family planning and human development are not fully accounted for. On the other hand, as fertility declines the world over, it is inevitable that a greater fraction of future growth will be attributable to the young age structure resulting from high levels of childbearing in the past—i.e., to population momentum. Therefore, policy options that address momentum will become increasingly critical.

[6] By this we mean the average age at which women bear children, not their mean age at first birth.

they have focused primarily on rites of passage at puberty rather than on socialization into procreative and economically productive roles (Bledsoe 1996). In part, this is because girls in most traditional cultures moved more or less directly from puberty into marriage and childbearing. A cross-cultural analysis of 46 preindustrial societies (based on ethnographic studies conducted between 1880 and 1980) found that many girls had no period of "maidenhood," defined as the interval between menarche and marriage. In 20 of these societies, girls were married at, or soon after, menarche, and sometimes moved into their future husband's residence even before reaching puberty. In the remaining 26 societies, marriage was delayed a maximum of four years following menarche (Whiting, Burbank, and Ratner 1986). Thus, to many observers, girls in such societies had no visible adolescence.[7]

The interval between puberty and marriage undoubtedly lasted longer for boys than for girls in preindustrial societies, as it does in traditional cultures today. In these settings, males generally need time to acquire resources before setting up a marital household and, therefore, do not marry until they are older—at which point they usually marry younger (often much younger) females (Caldwell et al. 1998). This accounts, at least in part, for the gender differential in the gap between puberty and marriage. Statements about the duration of this interval for males must remain speculative, however, because data on spermarche (the male equivalent of menarche) and men's age at marriage are extremely sparse (Whiting and Whiting 1990).

The consensus among social scientists is that adolescence as we know it—a period in which children attain physical maturity but are not burdened with adult roles and responsibilities—is an epiphenomenon of modern, industrial societies (Caldwell et al. 1998; Senderowitz 1995). Adolescence (from the Latin *adolescere*, to grow up) did not appear in the social science literature until 1904, when G. Stanley Hall published his two-volume work, *Adolescence: Its Psychology and Its Relations to Physiology, Anthropology, Sociology, Sex, Crime, Religion, and Education*. As early as the Middle Ages, however, the term was used to denote a stage in the life cycle of man (Kett 1971: 95).

---

[7] This was also true of girls in the United States prior to the twentieth century. The view that evolved in the nineteenth century was that only boys passed through a protracted stage of preparation for adult life following childhood (known as "youth," rather than "adolescence," at that time). Girls, on the other hand, moved from childhood through a brief, "wrenching" puberty (between the ages of about 14 and 16), and then were married promptly, if possible, to ward off the "threat to female virtue posed by the sudden onset of sexual maturity" (Kett 1971: 108). Marriage marked girls' entry into adulthood—a view that is still widely held today.

Recently, some anthropologists have criticized the historicization of adolescence, arguing that the stage between childhood dependency and adult autonomy is an inherent developmental phase, which exists in all cultures at all times (and even among other primates). In this view, adolescence always and everywhere involves the same set of issues: management of sexuality among unmarried individuals, social organization and peer group influence among adolescents, and training in occupational and life skills (Schlegel 1995). We agree with this conceptualization for the most part; however, we would modify it by arguing that adolescence does not end with marriage and/or childbearing. This is not a semantic fine point; it has important research and policy implications. The second decade of life is a time of heightened vulnerability for girls and critical capability-building for children of both sexes. These are defining features of adolescence; they apply to all 10–19-year-old children, regardless of their marital and/or childbearing status. This fact is obscured when we classify adolescent girls with husbands and/or children as "adults." Furthermore, this classification deprives such girls of the rights, protections, services, and opportunities afforded to other children their age. Thus, we maintain that a girl remains a girl until she reaches age 20, no matter what occurs in her life prior to that time.[8]

> **Adolescence does not end with marriage and/or childbearing.**

Current approaches to research on adolescents

Adolescents are gaining more attention from population researchers,[9] largely because of changing circumstances for girls in many countries. With education becoming more widespread,[10] age at marriage increasing (Singh and Samara 1996; Westoff, Blanc, and Nyblade 1994),[11] and age

---

[8] We include 19-year-olds in the category of children, although the Convention on the Rights of the Child defines them as adults.

[9] For example: the National Academy of Sciences' Committee on Population convened a workshop in March 1997 titled "Adolescent Sexuality and Reproductive Health in Developing Countries: Trends and Interventions" (see "Adolescent Reproductive Behavior in the Developing World," a special issue of *Studies in Family Planning*, 29, no. 2, 1998). A 1995 issue of *Population Reports* (which covers important developments in the population field) was devoted entirely to adolescence; it cited nearly 600 books and articles on the subject, culled from the population literature. Titled *Meeting the Needs of Young Adults*, the document defined these needs largely in relation to fertility and reproductive health (McCauley and Salter 1995).

[10] Surveys indicate an increase over the last 30 years in the percentage of women with some schooling. Moreover, female enrollment ratios for primary and secondary school (i.e., the number of girls of a given age enrolled in school compared to the number of children of that age in the population) also have risen, except in sub-Saharan Africa, where these numbers have stagnated over the last 15 years (McDevitt et al. 1996: 25–26, A16–A17).

[11] Evidence for this trend comes from a comparison of median ages at first marriage across birth cohorts for countries included in the Demographic and Health Sur-

> **Almost every major survey of adolescents to date lacks critical information on the background and context of sexual and reproductive behavior.**

at menarche declining (Barnes-Josiah and Augustin 1995; Cameron and Nagdee 1996; Chakravarty 1994; Jabbar and Wong 1988; Jaruratanasirikul and Lebel 1995; Sharma and Hiramani 1985), the interval between puberty and marriage is lengthening. As a result, girls in many parts of the world are facing a prolonged risk of pregnancy and reproductive health problems prior to marriage.

Most research on developing-country adolescents has taken a conventional approach to the study of sexual and reproductive behavior; thus, demographic data on adolescents are confined largely to the standard set of variables (e.g., percentage of females who marry and give birth before age 20). In response to the rising rates of HIV infection among teens, some recent studies have documented behaviors that jeopardize reproductive health. Unfortunately, data on adolescents are often collected only for females, and usually in limited age cohorts—for example, only teens aged 15–19 (see, for example, Alan Guttmacher Institute 1998; Loffredo et al. 1994; McCauley and Salter 1995; McDevitt et al. 1996; Noble, Cover, and Yanagishita 1996; Senderowitz 1995; WHO and UNICEF 1995).

The Demographic and Health Surveys (DHS) have served as the primary source of data for studies of developing-country adolescents by population researchers, with some notable exceptions (see, for example, Morris 1992, 1994). The DHS is principally designed to monitor the fertility and health behavior of females aged 15–49 (defined as "women of reproductive age") in more than 50 developing countries. Data from these surveys are indispensable for many purposes, but they are limited in ways that hamper research on adolescents. Their primary drawback also characterizes almost every major survey of adolescents to date: they lack critical information on the background and context of sexual and reproductive behavior. More specifically:

- There is insufficient time in the standard DHS interview to include probing questions about the behavior and circumstances of restricted age groups, despite the fact that events during the teen years can have profound implications for later life.
- Many of the surveys include too few 15–19-year-olds. This is because interviewers displace 15–16-year-olds out of the group eligible for individual interviews, and because older teenagers who do not know their own birthdate often say they are 20 years

---

veys. Retrospective reporting of age at marriage by older women (aged 40+) is considered less reliable because of recall error. When the comparison is restricted to women aged 20–39, the decline in median age at marriage is still apparent (except in many Latin American countries).

old, causing a "heaping on age 20" (Rutstein and Bicego 1990). Thus, it is unknown whether respondents reported to be 15–19 years old constitute a representative sample of teenagers in that age group.

- The DHS excludes girls under the age of 15, but many girls reach menarche sooner—some at age 10 or even earlier.

- In countries where female sexual activity and reproduction usually take place within marriage (about one-quarter of DHS countries), surveys are generally restricted to ever-married women; samples of adolescents are selective.[12] This exclusion of unmarried females provides an incomplete picture of adolescence in these countries.

- The DHS rarely interviews adolescent boys: out of 103 surveys, 46 have included males.[13] Until recently, these male respondents were limited to husbands of female respondents and other married men, most of them older than 20 (Macro International 1997).[14] Data on men are limited to such variables as numbers of living children, knowledge and use of contraceptives, fertility preferences, and knowledge and behavior related to AIDS (Ezeh, Seroussi, and Raggers 1996).

Other groups have conducted surveys of adolescents in several developing regions, but these efforts have also targeted reproductive behavior and health. For example:

- The East-West Center's Program on Population has undertaken surveys of adolescents in Hong Kong, the Philippines, and Thailand, and is planning surveys in Indonesia and Vietnam, as part of its program of research on youth sexuality. The surveys emphasize behaviors that put adolescents at risk of sexually transmitted infections (Balk, Cruz, and Brown 1997).[15]

- The U.S. Centers for Disease Control and Prevention (CDC) have been conducting a series of Young Adult Reproductive Health Surveys in eight Latin American and Caribbean coun-

---

[12] The countries where only currently married or ever-married women have been sampled are Bangladesh, Egypt, India, Indonesia, Jordan, Nepal, Pakistan, Sri Lanka, Sudan, Thailand, Tunisia, Turkey, and Yemen.

[13] These numbers exclude in-depth and experimental surveys.

[14] In the last five years, the DHS study design has been modified to include unmarried men. Adolescent boys aged 15–19, and sometimes even 12–19, have been included in 25 surveys. Of these, 21 were conducted in sub-Saharan Africa and four in Latin America and the Caribbean; thus, no surveys in Asia (East, South, or West) or North Africa include unmarried adolescent boys.

[15] Results of these surveys have not been published yet, but they have been presented at conferences.

tries. Their goal is to collect data on sexual activity and contraceptive use in a representative sample of youth, composed of 15–24-year-old males and females residing mostly in cities or island countries.[16] The surveys document premarital sexual activity, fertility, and contraceptive use (including use at first intercourse) without describing the environment in which these behaviors occur.[17]

- Surveys of African adolescents have been carried out by individual researchers, primarily in cities in Guinea, Kenya, Liberia, Nigeria, Senegal, and Zimbabwe. These surveys have many of the same limitations as the CDC surveys cited above (Ajayi et al. 1991; Amazigo et al. 1997; Boohene et al. 1991; Feyisetan and Pebley 1989; Görgen et al. 1998; Kiragu and Zabin 1993; Naré, Katz, and Tolley 1996; Nichols et al. 1986; Nichols et al. 1987; Youri 1994).

A few studies of adolescents have obtained some of the background and contextual information that is notably lacking from the surveys cited above:

- The 1995 Yaoundé Family Formation Dynamics Study examined the context of sexual activity in a group of single 17–25-year-old males and females in the capital of Cameroon. Using a structured survey and focus groups, the researchers examined the motivations and strategies underlying the subjects' sexual relationships. Given its focus and the age of its subjects, this study belongs more to the literature on sexual networking (which arose in response to the AIDS crisis) than to the literature on adolescence, but it could serve as a model for studies of adolescents (Calvès, Cornwell, and Enyegue 1996; Orubuloye et al. 1994).

- A series of studies conducted by the International Center for Research on Women examined the nutritional status of adolescents in Benin, Cameroon, Ecuador, Guatemala, India, Jamaica, Mexico, Nepal, and the Philippines. In several countries, researchers asked respondents what they did while awake (because daily activity affects caloric requirements). Although the time-use data were flawed by the inaccuracies of retrospec-

---

[16] The survey in Jamaica used age 14 as the lower boundary. One national survey was conducted in Costa Rica.

[17] This is predictable, given that the surveys were modeled on the U.S. Youth Risk Behavior Surveillance System, which collects data on unsafe and often illegal behaviors, such as unprotected sex and drug use (Morris 1992, 1994; Morris, Warren, and Aral 1993).

tive recall (Bouis 1996), the data did provide some insight into quotidian aspects of adolescents' lives (Kurz and Johnson-Welch 1994).

- A recent study of adolescents in Egypt represents the most comprehensive effort to overcome the shortcomings of previous surveys. In 1997, researchers conducted a nationally representative survey of more than 9,000 Egyptian girls and boys aged 10–19. They collected information on education, work roles, social integration and emotional wellbeing, and daily activities. For a subset of the sample, data were collected on gender dynamics in the natal household, expectations regarding future roles and responsibilities within marriage, marriage and fertility behavior, general health and nutrition (including a clinical assessment), and reproductive health knowledge and attitudes (El-Tawila et al. 1998; Ibrahim, Mensch, and El Gibaly 1998).[18]

Overall, however, studies in developing countries have left us with a dearth of data on 10–19-year-olds, especially younger and unmarried ones. We are missing basic demographic and health information on many adolescents; we know little about their age- and gender-specific life experiences; we cannot identify the key transition points in their development; and we know few of the differentiating characteristics of married/unmarried and sexually active/inactive adolescents.

Some voices in the population field have called for data collection efforts devoted exclusively to capturing adolescents' experiences in developing countries.[19] This research could be made more multi-dimensional if it were to follow the course of research on adolescents in the United States, which has widened its scope in recent decades. While most of the U.S. work has focused on fertility,[20] more and more studies are looking at other aspects of adolescents' lives, including work, joblessness, and wages (D'Amico and Maxwell 1992; Gill and Michaels 1992; Grogger 1992; Kaestner 1991; Klerman and Karoly 1994; Michael and Tuma 1984; Mortimer et al. 1990; Powers 1994; Wolpin

> **Research on developing-country adolescents could be made more multi-dimensional if it were to follow the course of research on adolescents in the United States.**

---

[18] This ongoing study is a collaborative effort involving the Social Research Center of the American University in Cairo, the Population Council regional office for West Asia and North Africa, the High Institute for Public Health of Alexandria University, and the Department of Community Medicine at Assiut University.

[19] Leo Morris, the demographer with the most experience fielding surveys of adolescents in developing countries, argued in a session at the National Academy of Sciences workshop on developing-country adolescents (see footnote 9) that donors should fund data collection efforts in this area if they really want to understand what is going on in this segment of the population.

[20] In the 1970s and 1980s, studies of adolescents in the United States focused primarily on sexuality and pregnancy, as researchers sought to explain the disturbingly high

> **Our analytic and policy bias is to pay closest attention to the antecedents of adolescent fertility and poor reproductive health.**

1992);[21] education (Mensch and Kandel 1988; Sandefur, McLanahan, and Wojtkiewicz 1992; Veum and Weiss 1993; Wojtkiewicz 1993); gender role attitudes (Ortiz and Cooney 1984); and place of residence (Haurin 1992).[22] These topics need to be explored in research on developing-country adolescents. This is true whether the policy concern driving this research remains the reduction of adolescent pregnancy and reproductive health problems, or whether it shifts—as we would hope—to a broader concern with human rights and human development.

Our analytic approach

The demographic and health consequences of adolescent reproductive behavior, which have been defined by the population field as subjects of primary interest, concern us as well; but our analytic and policy bias is to pay closest attention to the antecedents of adolescent fertility and poor reproductive health. Adolescent sexual initiation and fertility are certainly significant demographic and epidemiological events, but they result from social, economic, and gender dynamics deeply rooted in family systems, peer relationships, and societal institutions. Thus, adolescent sexual and reproductive behavior cannot be explained and modified without understanding the familial and societal forces that shape this

---

rates of premarital childbearing in the country (see, for example, Hayes 1987; Jones et al. 1989; Zelnik, Kantner, and Ford 1981). In recent years, studies have shifted their focus to the high rates of unintended pregnancy among younger and older females (Brown and Eisenberg 1995). A recent review of the literature on adolescents goes so far as to criticize the so-called "inventors of adolescent pregnancy," who view teenage pregnancy as an individual failing rather than as a socially constructed, structural problem (Nathanson 1991: 223). The widely held belief that early childbearing has deleterious consequences has also come under attack in the United States. The inability to control for selection effects (i.e., the fact that teenage mothers are different from those who delay childbearing to begin with) has made it difficult to sort out causes and effects of early childbearing (Luker 1996). Some would argue that if teen pregnancy were eliminated, the impoverished environment in which such pregnancy often occurs would not be transformed, nor would the life of those mired in such settings be markedly improved.

[21] A notable data collection effort in the United States was the National Longitudinal Survey of Youth (NLSY), launched in 1979 by the U.S. Department of Labor's Bureau of Labor Statistics in response to concerns about adolescent labor force participation. The NLSY, which surveyed 12,686 male and female youth aged 14–22 (when first interviewed), is an enormously rich data set that includes information on educational progress and performance, school environment, time use, relationships with parents, peer networks, drug and alcohol use, health, personality characteristics, occupational and educational aspirations, gender role attitudes, and work histories. It also contains the standard items on sexual behavior, contraceptive use, pregnancy, abortion, and marriage. The NLSY has no parallel in the developing world (Card 1993; Center for Human Resource Research 1994). While the authors cited in the text who use NLSY data are all members of the Population Association of America, they would not universally label themselves demographers or population specialists, which may explain their interest in more than demographic data.

behavior. We therefore explore how girls are treated in their families, schools, peer groups, and communities; and we probe for evidence of girls' exclusion from, or integration into, the social and economic mainstream of their societies.

In preparing this monograph, our task was twofold: finding and then interpreting the data on female (and, to some extent, male) adolescents in developing countries. We reviewed the relevant literature; then, from the fragments of available information, we reconstructed girls' passage from age 10 to 19 in developing countries.

Given the scarcity of data on adolescent girls, we are only able to present illustrative statistics in our analysis. Where data exist on boys, comparisons are made. We draw on conventional fertility surveys as well as other types of research—for example, studies of nutrition, time use, and family structure—to obtain a broad picture of girls' lives. For the most part, we rely on the 39 Demographic and Health Surveys conducted since 1990 for which data were available in mid-1998.[23] These surveys represent 53 percent of the population of Latin America and the Caribbean; 31 percent of the population of South Central and Southeast Asia; 77 percent of the population of sub-Saharan Africa; and 50 percent of the population of West Asia and North Africa.[24] Disproportionately more sub-Saharan African countries are included simply because more surveys were conducted in this region.

In our work, we share the orientation of those in the child welfare and development community who have moved beyond the concern with young children's mere survival to the question: Survival for what? This question raises the issue of young people's capabilities, rights, and quality of life—a vital addition to the discourse on human development.

At present, public policy is marked by a radical discontinuity. Between infant/child survival programs and maternal–child health/family planning programs, conventional development efforts go into laten-

---

[22] Dryfoos (1990), one of the leading experts on teen pregnancy in the United States, now argues that a fragmented approach to youth problems is wasteful of resources. She maintains that delinquency, substance abuse, pregnancy, and failure in school arise from a common set of social and familial conditions; therefore, efforts should focus more on improving these conditions and less on preventing specific behaviors. Nathanson (1991) agrees.

[23] For some subjects, data do not exist for all 39 countries. These countries are excluded from tables presenting these data.

[24] We use these regional headings throughout, except where we present findings from research in which other headings were used. We use the Population Reference Bureau (1997) regional heading "South Central and Southeast Asia" because we present data from Asian countries that do not belong under the more common headings South Asia or East Asia.

> **We follow adolescent girls along the path of their development, from their childhood homes out into the larger contexts of their lives—school, work, the sexual and reproductive realm.**

cy. Girls disappear as policy subjects after receiving their last childhood immunization and do not reappear until they are pregnant and, in most cases, married. Fortunately, this is beginning to change as school enrollment becomes a higher-profile policy issue,[25] calling attention to the needs of youth aged 5–18. Even so, adolescents (and, indeed, children over age 5) remain neglected from a policy point of view.

In the next two chapters, we follow adolescent girls along the path of their development, from their childhood homes out into the larger contexts of their lives—school, work, the sexual and reproductive realm—charting their experience in these areas. We recognize that there are "enormous differences across the world in adolescent sexuality, reproduction, and marriage" (Caldwell et al. 1998: 137); but there are also patterns of experience common to many girls in developing countries, which have not been emphasized in the literature. Our aim is to describe these patterns in order to provide researchers and policymakers with a broad, flexible framework for understanding girls' experience.[26] In the final chapter, we offer an agenda for adolescent policy, programs, and research. We hope this effort will help to generate more interest in adolescent girls—indeed, all adolescents—and more inspiration to improve their lives.

---

[25] At the 1995 World Summit for Social Development, in Copenhagen, primary school attendance was identified as an issue in need of special attention.

[26] We leave it to others to explain the origin of differences in girls' experience from place to place, many of which are rooted in "precontact culture" (Caldwell et al. 1998: 151), and to adapt our framework to fit the unique conditions that prevail in specific settings.

Chapter 2

The Social and Economic Context of Girls' Adolescence: Home, School, and Work

In this chapter we discuss the social and economic context of adolescent girls' lives in developing countries, focusing on areas of their experience that have been largely neglected by researchers and policymakers. These include girls' living arrangements; domestic roles and responsibilities; social and physical mobility; schooling; and work. These factors are critical to girls' wellbeing, social power, and ability to set the terms of sexual relations and childbearing. They also reflect girls' status within their families and communities. We argue that the conventional sexual and reproductive variables (discussed in Chapter 3) are, to a large extent, outcomes of this status. In the sections below, we summarize what is currently known about each subject, offer relevant data from the Demographic and Health Surveys and other sources, and suggest information that would be useful to collect in the future.

Living arrangements

In order to get a clear picture of adolescents' lives, it is vital to know where they live and what their status is within their household: whether they are being supported and by whom, whether they are rendering services, and so forth. The few programmatic efforts to engage adolescents typically presuppose some permanence in their living situation and some reliable point of catchment; for example, adolescents are generally assumed to be living with their parents. Such assumptions may be mistaken.

The scarcity of data on adolescent living arrangements partly reflects the difficulty of obtaining data on families, as opposed to households, and the tendency to define household status, wealth, and wellbeing according to characteristics of the nominal head of household, usually identified as the eldest adult male (Bruce and Lloyd 1997). The DHS data on survivorship and residence of parents—a clue to adolescent living arrangements—are available only for children under age 15.

The existing data suggest that adolescent living situations vary substantially between developing countries. In Asian countries, such as Pakistan and Turkey, 3–4 percent of boys and girls aged 12–14 live in a household without either parent (see Table 1). These percentages are three or more times higher for both sexes—9–36 percent for boys and 12–42 percent for girls—in all of the Caribbean, Latin American, and sub-Saharan African countries in Table 1.

A substantial proportion of both girls and boys live in households without a father. Percentages range from 6 to 15 percent in Asia and North Africa to about 25 percent in some African and Latin American countries (see Table 1). As children get older, their risk increases of living in a household with only one parent, usually the mother. A 10–14-year-old is about 3 percent more likely than a 5–9-year-old to live in such a household in Asia, Latin America, and North Africa (Lloyd and Desai 1992); this risk is likely to be even higher for 15–19-year-olds. Living with a single parent may have a disproportionately negative impact on girls, given that domestic responsibilities are usually transferred to daughters rather than to sons (see discussion under "Domestic roles and responsibilities"). Girls in single-parent households, particularly older daughters, may miss out on schooling opportunities because they must stay at home to care for younger siblings. Given that the proportion of single-parent households is rising throughout the world (Bruce, Lloyd, and Leonard 1995), this problem could affect an increasing share of girls in developing countries.

Sub-Saharan Africa is a special case with respect to adolescent living arrangements. In the countries in this region shown in Table 1, 18–42 percent of 12–14-year-old girls live in a household without either parent. In Benin, Côte d'Ivoire, Ghana, and Niger, considerably more girls than boys live in such households.[1] Presumably many of these girls have been "fostered out"—that is, sent to live with another family. The rationale that parents present for having their children live away, apart from this being a cultural practice, is that it may improve their children's status. For example, moving to an urban household may bring a girl more amenities and opportunities to learn an urban language, meet wealthy suitors, and attend school (Bledsoe and Isiugo-Abanihe 1989).

---

[1] Many more girls than boys live without either parent in two Caribbean countries as well: the Dominican Republic and Haiti (see Table 1). We cannot determine the reason for this from the limited data available.

TABLE 1
Percentage of Unmarried Adolescents Aged 12–14 Living in Households Without Either Parent or Without a Father

Region/Country	Without either parent		Without a father	
	Girls	Boys	Girls	Boys
Latin America and the Caribbean				
Brazil*	12	9	18	18
Colombia*	14	13	25	25
Dominican Republic	27	18	20	22
Guatemala	9	8	17	17
Haiti	36	26	22	23
Paraguay	17	12	11	14
South Central and Southeast Asia				
Indonesia*	9	7	7	9
Kazakstan	10	5	15	15
Pakistan*	4	4	8	7
Philippines	11	9	7	8
Uzbekistan	2	2	8	6
Sub-Saharan Africa				
Benin	33	19	13	11
Burkina Faso	21	16	7	7
Cameroon	26	24	12	13
Central African Republic	28	25	17	15
Comoros	28	23	27	26
Côte d'Ivoire	36	25	14	12
Ghana*	30	20	23	26
Kenya	19	15	25	25
Madagascar	22	21	17	16
Mali	18	11	8	8
Namibia	42	36	24	22
Niger	26	16	10	7
Nigeria	22	16	11	18
Senegal	21	20	17	16
Tanzania	23	22	18	18
Uganda	31	27	18	18
Zambia*	28	25	18	17
Zimbabwe	27	24	24	27
West Asia and North Africa				
Morocco	8	9	10	10
Turkey*	3	3	7	6

* Marital status of adolescents is known. In all other countries, marital status is unknown; adolescents are assumed to be unmarried.

Source: Computations from DHS household data since 1990. See Appendix for survey dates.

Reality often belies this scenario, however. Increasingly, studies suggest that some (perhaps many) foster children, particularly girls, end up as unpaid and ill-treated domestic servants, subjected to "beating[s], enforced hard labor [and] food deprivation" (Bledsoe 1990). In an analysis of the economic rationale for child fostering in Côte d'Ivoire (based on World Bank living standards data), Ainsworth concludes that her "findings are consistent with a child labor explanation and inconclusive with respect to schooling investments as a motive [for fostering]." She reports that "foster girls perform housework. . .while boys are engaged in production of marketed agricultural goods." Supporting the observation that foster children contribute to household labor, she also notes that there are "far more economic determinants of fostering on the demand side (fostering in) than on the supply side (fostering out)" (Ainsworth 1996: 25, 45, 53).

The causal relationship between adolescents' living arrangements and their school status cannot be determined with simple DHS tabulations, in part because the reasons that children live away from home vary widely. Taken at face value, DHS data indicate that fostering certainly does not increase school enrollment and may sometimes actually reduce it. In countries where at least 10 percent of 12–14-year-olds live away from both parents, school enrollment in this group is equally likely to be lower (as in Kenya) or higher (as in Benin) than enrollment among children of the same age who live with both parents (see Table 2).

UNICEF reports that there is a growing distrust of fostering arrangements: "families nowadays are leery of sending [their children] to people who merely keep them for domestic training and do not teach them a trade or send them to school" (UNICEF 1997: 137). It is unknown, however, whether this reported change in attitude toward fostering has actually reduced the frequency of the practice.

This review of the limited data on living arrangements challenges the assumption that all adolescents reliably can be found at home and under the care of parents or other adults. Systematic efforts to get a picture of where adolescent girls live (particularly the youngest ones), and whether and by whom they are supported, are called for. So, too, are studies of the risks that particular living arrangements pose to adolescent girls. These data are essential for planning interventions for these girls, whether such measures are designed to improve school enrollment rates, to free up more of girls' time for study, or to protect them from exploitative arrangements.

Domestic roles and responsibilities

Adolescent girls' homes are not just residential bases; they are also the loci of powerful familial forces that shape every aspect of girls' existence, including their time use, access to school and paid work, and social status. Many adolescent girls are virtually entrapped in the domestic sphere. This confinement serves two purposes: it keeps girls out of the public arena (see "Social and physical mobility") and it keeps them in

TABLE 2

Percentage of Unmarried Adolescents Aged 12–14 Currently Attending School in Households With Both Parents, Without a Father, or Without Either Parent

Region/Country	With both parents		Without a father		Without either parent	
	Girls	Boys	Girls	Boys	Girls	Boys
Latin America and the Caribbean						
Brazil	94	93	92	93	89	93
Colombia	87	84	72	68	84	82
Dominican Republic	92	87	86	80	85	73
Haiti	84	84	88	86	71	77
Paraguay	74	84	69	83	71	80
South Central and Southeast Asia						
Kazakstan	99	99	99	100	100	98
Uzbekistan	99	98	96	100	97	92
Sub-Saharan Africa						
Benin	34	57	18	55	44	60
Burkina Faso	16	30	20	38	37	41
Cameroon	68	76	80	94	73	74
Central African Republic	54	73	34	68	45	70
Comoros	64	80	55	69	61	76
Côte d'Ivoire	47	58	29	55	45	63
Ghana	68	73	77	82	70	85
Kenya	91	92	95	94	76	81
Madagascar	56	67	45	43	46	50
Malawi	73	75	52	65	63	69
Mali	21	33	19	37	28	44
Namibia	94	93	94	88	97	94
Niger	14	28	11	28	15	25
Nigeria	53	65	69	100	67	27
Senegal	27	37	32	51	27	44
Tanzania	80	79	70	70	79	82
Uganda	75	86	67	74	64	75
Zambia	78	80	69	70	74	71
Zimbabwe	92	91	92	90	82	87

Source: Computations from DHS household data since 1990 for countries where at least 10 percent of 12–14-year-olds of either sex live apart from both parents. See Appendix for survey dates.

the household, where they undergo their apprenticeship for adulthood—an intense training for a lifelong role as wife and mother.

In preparation for marriage, girls are generally encouraged to be docile and compliant members of the family. They are often expected to assist mothers and other female relatives with domestic duties, such as child care, food preparation, and other time-consuming activities, including the fetching of water and fuel, cleaning, and agricultural work (see, for example, Kiem 1993). They may have sole responsibility for some of these chores: in Bangladesh, many girls do all of the cooking for their family. Older girls may be restricted to indoor tasks: while "young

Girls carry a greater domestic work burden than boys in virtually every country where data are available.

[Bangladeshi] girls usually engage in off-*bari* (home) activities, such as fuel collection and tending animals, adolescent girls are constrained by *purdah* to work in and around the home" (Amin 1996: 194).

In contrast to girls, boys are encouraged to develop some degree of autonomy and independence from the family, even in societies that stress filial obedience; this situation is remarkably consistent throughout the developing world (Amin 1996; Devasia and Devasia 1991; Kiem 1993; Maher 1974; Phillips 1973; Williams 1968). Not surprisingly, studies indicate that girls carry a greater domestic work burden than boys in virtually every country where data are available (Ajayi et al. 1997; Bouis et al. 1997; Cain 1977; Lloyd and Gage 1995).[2] This gender disparity emerges relatively early in childhood, with girls devoting considerably more hours to housework and boys engaging in more "productive" activities that generate income. Qualitative studies conclude that most girls spend more time working and have measurably less leisure time than boys (Alexander 1991; Cain 1977; Kiem 1993; Minge-Klevana 1980; Pantelides, Geldstein, and Dominguez 1995; Phillips 1973). This inequity reflects girls' and boys' differential roles and status within the family and community. (For more on girls' and boys' relative workloads, see "Work").

The pressure of domestic work would appear to constrain girls' access to schooling and their ability to concentrate on their studies. The literature on gender differences in educational participation suggests that girls' household and child care responsibilities may compete with school attendance and interfere with homework (Herz et al. 1991). Attending school certainly does not exempt girls from domestic chores: as an 18-year-old girl in North India noted, "If you study you have to make *roti*, and if you don't study you have to make *roti*" (Jeffery and Jeffery 1996: 150). Recent data from Kenya, where the school day is often quite long,[3] indicate that schoolgirls spend an average of almost two hours a day on domestic duties, while schoolboys spend less than one hour a day on such tasks. Interestingly, there is near parity in the time devoted to homework (Ajayi et al. 1997). In settings where double school shifts are common, or school occupies only a few hours a day, we may expect to see a greater gap between the hours that girls and boys dedicate to work in and around the home.

---

[2] Even in highly industrialized countries, such as Australia, Canada, and the United States, girls do more domestic work than boys in many families (Sohoni 1995).

[3] In a sample of 36 primary schools in three districts, representing the range of schools in Kenya, the average school day is eight hours in the 28 single-shift schools, and four hours in the eight double-shift schools (Mensch and Lloyd 1998).

The disparity between girls' and boys' domestic workloads is most striking among adolescents who are not in school. In Kenya, out-of-school girls perform more than eight times as much domestic work as out-of-school boys: girls aged 12–19 average 6 hours and 49 minutes and boys of that age average 49 minutes a day (Ajayi et al. 1997). In Bangladesh, where the difference between girls' and boys' contributions to domestic work is more modest, the greatest workload differential is also between out-of-school boys and girls: 16–19-year-old boys average 12 minutes a day on domestic tasks, whereas girls of the same age average 5 hours a day—25 times more work. Although their domestic burden is light, 16–19-year-old Bangladeshi boys who are out of school average 2.3 hours a day on wage work; however, this is still less time than girls spend on domestic tasks (Arends-Kuenning, Sedgh, and Amin 1998).[4]

Even in settings outside the home, girls may do disproportionately more "domestic" work, reflecting the persistence of this gender role. In Guinea and Kenya, girls are more likely than boys to perform menial chores in school, such as preparing and serving food or cleaning the classroom (Anderson-Levitt, Bloch, and Soumaré 1998; Mensch and Lloyd 1998). Female participation in a sports program in Kenya included the expectation that girl soccer players would wash boys' uniforms (Brady 1997).[5]

Girls' play appears to be designed to accommodate their domestic tasks. Girls are expected to remain close to home when they play so that they can still care for younger siblings and be on call to meet the demands of their elders. In contrast, adolescent boys appear to spend more time playing with their peers away from home, out of the reach of family responsibilities (Jain 1988; LeVine et al. 1994; Maher 1974; Mandelbaum 1988).

Girls' familial roles and responsibilities bind them to the domestic sphere, where they are expected to spend most of their lives, first as daughters, then as wives and mothers. Girls who never move beyond this domain may be considered successful from a traditional perspective, but their "success" often comes at a steep, personal price, as the discussion below shows.

Social and physical mobility

Adolescent girls' ability to move beyond their home and family-defined identity has profound implications for their development. Girls'

---

[4] Data are drawn from Amin's 1995–96 survey titled "Family Structure and Change in Rural Bangladesh."

[5] Following a "gender training" session, this practice was discontinued.

autonomy and skill levels are substantially limited if they are not at liberty to leave home to visit friends, places, or institutions outside the family; participate in female solidarity groups; and identify themselves publicly as students, workers, and citizens.

In many developing countries, adolescent girls' mobility is highly constrained.[6] Restrictions placed on girls are generally put forward as an effort to protect rather than harm them. Concerns about girls' sexuality and sexual safety are commonly invoked as the rationale for monitoring their movements outside the home. From Latin America to South Asia, girls' "protectors" express a general distrust of men, including male relatives (Mandelbaum 1988; Tenorio, Farrín, and Bonilla 1995).

Restricting a girl's mobility may or may not protect her from sexual harm, but it does protect the status of her family. In many cultures, the terms of a girl's marriage and sexual initiation are considered emblematic; thus, family honor is at stake in every encounter between an adolescent girl and a male. Even when girls are freed from the confines of home, they are often required to follow strict rules of public comportment. They may be expected to demonstrate discomfort with the world outside the home; for example, bold or direct looks may be strongly discouraged (Aziz 1989; Phillips 1973; Romero 1988; Williams 1968).

Economic considerations may reshape families' expectations of girls. In rural areas, adolescent girls may be required to do outside work, such as laboring in fields or washing clothes in streams. While this may give them "inappropriate" visibility and contact with males, it may also give them slightly more authority and independence than their female counterparts in better-off families (Aziz 1989; Jain 1988; Kanhere 1989; Mandelbaum 1988; Miller 1981; Ullrich 1977). In some settings, economic necessity may even soften the observance of menstrual taboos, which would ordinarily restrict older girls and women to the household

---

[6] Comparative data on girls' and boys' mobility are not available. To obtain an indirect measure of their relative mobility, we used household composition data in 42 DHS country reports for surveys since 1990 to compute urban, rural, and aggregate sex ratios (boys to girls) in five-year age groups of 10–24-year-olds (data not shown). If an urban sex ratio were considerably higher and a rural sex ratio were considerably lower than 1.0, it would suggest that boys were more likely than girls to move to urban areas. However, among those aged 15–19 and 20–24, sex ratios in both areas are often so low that the data are of questionable validity: in ten countries, the aggregate sex ratio in these groups is .90 or lower, and in 15 countries the urban ratio is also that low. In Bangladesh, a country where purdah limits the movement of girls, the urban sex ratio is .85 among 15–19-year-olds and .69 among 20–24-year-olds. That boys appear to be "missing" from cities in Bangladesh is not an indication that they are less likely to migrate than girls; rather, it suggests that young males are not being captured in household surveys, perhaps *because* they are so mobile, and also because they are more likely to be in institutional settings, such as the army.

compound at times when they are wanted in the fields (Ullrich 1977). However, in other places, including Bangladesh, Pakistan, and parts of India, the desire to confine girls and women as a mark of status is so great that families with sufficient resources often prefer to limit females' mobility "because of the loss of prestige associated with working outside the home" (Amin 1996: 185; see also Papanek 1982).

The control of girls' time and movements would appear to restrict their emergence as individuals and to maintain familial authority over their lives. We can only infer this, however, as there are no systematic studies that explicitly examine adolescent girls' and boys' involvement in the public sphere. We know that girls are not encouraged to engage in community development efforts; we also know that they are excluded from governmental processes and policies through which citizenship is formally recognized. In many parts of the world, older adolescent boys must join the military, which offers them the important asset of an identity card and often provides them with productive skills (though the costs of training boys to be soldiers may frequently outweigh the benefits). Publicly mandated rites of passage for girls (ideally nonmilitary ones), which could offer public recognition of their having achieved social seniority, are absent in most societies.

Where opportunities are purposefully structured to engage young people, they usually attract more boys than girls. This is probably the result of a combination of factors: girls' heavy domestic burden, parental resistance to daughters' participation, and girls' discomfort in a male-dominated environment. An evaluation of youth centers in urban Kenya and Zimbabwe revealed that in two two-week periods in 1996 and 1997, adolescent male visitors outnumbered females by more than 2 to 1; the speculation was that girls were intimidated by the predominantly "male atmosphere" (Erulkar and Mensch 1997b; Phiri and Erulkar 1997).[7] A popular youth sports association with over 10,000 members in the slums of Nairobi had an impressive number of girls involved—2,500—yet three times as many boys participated (Brady 1997). The soccer league staff reported that organizing leagues for girls was a difficult challenge, given that even young girls have heavy family responsibilities (MYSA 1996).

> The control of girls' time and movements would appear to restrict their emergence as individuals and to maintain familial authority over their lives.

---

[7] The fact that the youth centers were under the auspices of family planning programs also may have branded them unfavorably in the minds of girls and their parents. Two of three centers run by the National Family Planning Council in Zimbabwe did attract proportionately more females, but the absolute numbers of female visitors were small. Furthermore, more than half of them were aged 20 or older—that is, they were young women seeking family planning services rather than adolescent girls seeking recreational activities, few of which were offered at these centers. The third center (in Mutare), which offers more recreational activities and has as library, attracted many more adolescents—3,000 in the two-week period compared to 250 at each of the other two centers—but the vast majority of these visitors were boys.

Increasing girls' participation in activities outside the home is not just a question of scheduling; it is a matter of renegotiating girls' social position. A community development program in Maqattam, a poor area on the outskirts of Cairo, which gave special attention to the social and economic potential of girls aged 10–20, found that bargaining with families over scheduling amounted to "negotiations over the family's view of this child" (Assaad and Bruce 1997: 18). By working closely with families to realign girls' responsibilities, the project "demonstrated that, with slight adjustments in 'scheduling,' a girl can suddenly move beyond the world of mother-father-sister-brother to one of studies, teachers, trainers, managers of income-generating programs, and the world beyond Maqattam . . ." (Assaad and Bruce 1997: 18). In rural Zimbabwe, where boys outnumber girls in secondary school by 6 to 1, the Cambridge Female Education Trust Project, established to encourage girls' secondary school attendance, recruited girls in community-based groups; in essence, they created girls' solidarity groups, which brought more gender balance to the classroom and provided girls with crucial social support (Cotton 1996).

Investigators who study women's status often emphasize the role of social mobility in improving women's self-regard; in offering women an independent, public identity; and in providing them with a practical base from which to press for change (Sanday 1974). Some of the same thinking should be applied in considering the experience of adolescent girls and assessing what it would take to improve their status.

Schooling

To the extent that governments acknowledge a sense of responsibility to adolescents, it is generally expressed through policies that extend schooling into the teen years. Most developing countries have compulsory schooling regulations. Of 103 countries in Africa, Asia, Latin America, and the Middle East for which UNESCO provides data, 12 mandate four or five years of schooling; 33 mandate six years; 23 mandate seven or eight years; and 35 mandate nine to 12 years. That is, just about half require children to go to school through at least age 14, assuming they began at age 6 (UNESCO 1997).

Table 3 shows the percentage of adolescents attending school by age and sex in 39 countries where the DHS was conducted since 1990. There are several patterns to note. In 33 of these countries, the majority of 12–13-year-old girls and boys are in school. In 24 of the countries, at least 5 percent more boys than girls are attending school. In one country, the Dominican Republic, at least 5 percent more girls than boys are

TABLE 3
Percentage of Adolescents Attending School by Age and Sex

Region/Country	Age 12–13 Girls	Boys	Age 14–15 Girls	Boys	Age 16–17 Girls	Boys	Age 18–19 Girls	Boys
Latin America and the Caribbean								
Bolivia	82	90	68	79	54	67	38	50
Brazil	95	94	85	85	69	67	48	44
Colombia	86	85	75	71	63	57	42	41
Dominican Republic	88	83	83	76	66	58	48	34
Guatemala	62	74	45	51	35	36	22	31
Haiti	78	83	81	81	69	77	53	68
Paraguay	82	90	50	60	36	41	27	24
Peru	89	90	82	85	68	71	49	53
South Central and Southeast Asia								
Bangladesh	66	67	40	52	26	46	17	34
Indonesia	79	82	57	65	38	44	19	27
Kazakstan	99	99	93	90	49	40	31	25
Nepal	51	77	44	68	27	50	14	34
Pakistan	44	69	35	61	23	48	13	33
Philippines	93	90	84	81	66	62	45	45
Uzbekistan	99	99	91	92	39	44	17	15
Sub-Saharan Africa								
Benin	29	57	30	49	21	40	6	27
Burkina Faso	21	34	15	24	11	19	9	17
Cameroon	71	77	64	72	47	65	28	42
Central African Republic	43	71	44	64	23	50	13	35
Comoros	59	76	57	74	51	64	38	54
Côte d'Ivoire	41	60	34	53	19	42	13	31
Ghana	74	81	60	71	35	54	15	39
Kenya	90	91	83	88	62	71	26	49
Madagascar	55	63	35	38	18	24	12	13
Malawi	63	72	60	66	36	61	17	48
Mali	21	35	19	29	12	24	8	20
Namibia	94	92	91	88	77	83	51	65
Niger	13	29	9	18	7	13	6	12
Nigeria	59	68	45	57	35	45	22	38
Rwanda	55	57	32	36	15	23	10	13
Senegal	30	45	19	31	12	23	9	23
Tanzania	77	77	71	71	36	51	11	23
Uganda	70	80	59	73	26	54	12	36
Zambia	79	78	61	71	40	59	17	40
Zimbabwe	93	91	72	83	46	66	17	34
West Asia and North Africa								
Egypt	69	77	63	71	55	65	29	41
Morocco	38	58	31	47	26	37	17	28
Turkey	53	76	41	58	25	45	15	25
Yemen	36	92	25	87	21	78	14	58

Source: Computations from DHS household data since 1990. See Appendix for survey dates.

attending. There are only 10 countries—six in Latin America—in which over half of 16–17-year-olds are in school, and only in Namibia are at least three-quarters of children of this age in school.

As a general pattern, girls' school enrollment lags behind boys'—but there are striking regional differences and some exceptions. Girls' enrollment actually exceeds boys' in several Latin American countries and in the Philippines (Herz et al. 1991; Hill and King 1993). Analyses of UNESCO and World Bank data from 81 countries indicate that the gender gap in enrollment rates is much higher for secondary than for primary school in all regions except Latin America and in the Philippines.[8] As a percentage of male enrollment, female enrollment declines between primary and secondary school in 25 of 29 African countries; 10 of 15 Asian countries; 11 of 17 Middle Eastern countries; but only 1 of 20 Latin American countries (derived from appendix to Table 3 in Herz et al. 1991). In a number of African countries—most prominently Cameroon, Ghana, Uganda, and Zimbabwe—girls' school enrollment decreases much more sharply than boys' between ages 12 and 17. These data reveal that, with respect to school enrollment, adolescence is a particularly vulnerable period for African girls.

DHS school attendance data and UNESCO enrollment figures lead to similar conclusions about gender differentials in school participation. Figure 1, which graphs girls' attendance as a percentage of boys' for 39 DHS countries grouped by region, illustrates that the gender gap in school attendance increases markedly during adolescence in sub-Saharan Africa and also increases in Asia and North Africa, although less sharply.[9] For example, in Tanzania there is no gender gap in attendance among 12–13-year-olds, but among 16–17-year-olds the gap is quite large (girls' attendance is only 71 percent of boys'). In Indonesia, the gender gap is virtually nonexistent among 12–13-year-olds (girls'

---

[8] To compare school participation in developing countries, many researchers rely on UNESCO's gross enrollment ratios—the number of children of any age enrolled at a certain level of school divided by the number of children in the population of the appropriate age for that level (see, for example, Bongaarts and Cohen 1998; Hill and King 1993). These ratios are not accurate indicators of school participation for two reasons: 1) many children enter school at a late age and repeat grades; and 2) the numerator is based on enrollment data provided to education ministries by school authorities at local and district levels, and since the resources allocated to these authorities are based on enrollment levels, there is an incentive to inflate enrollment figures. A comparison of UNESCO enrollment ratios and school attendance rates from DHS surveys in sub-Saharan Africa indicates that population-based attendance rates are almost always lower—often substantially lower—than those implied by gross enrollment ratios (Lloyd, Kaufman, and Hewett 1998). In this paragraph we summarize findings from studies based on UNESCO data because these data are available for a large number of countries. However, the education data presented in tables and figures are based on DHS data because those data are more accurate.

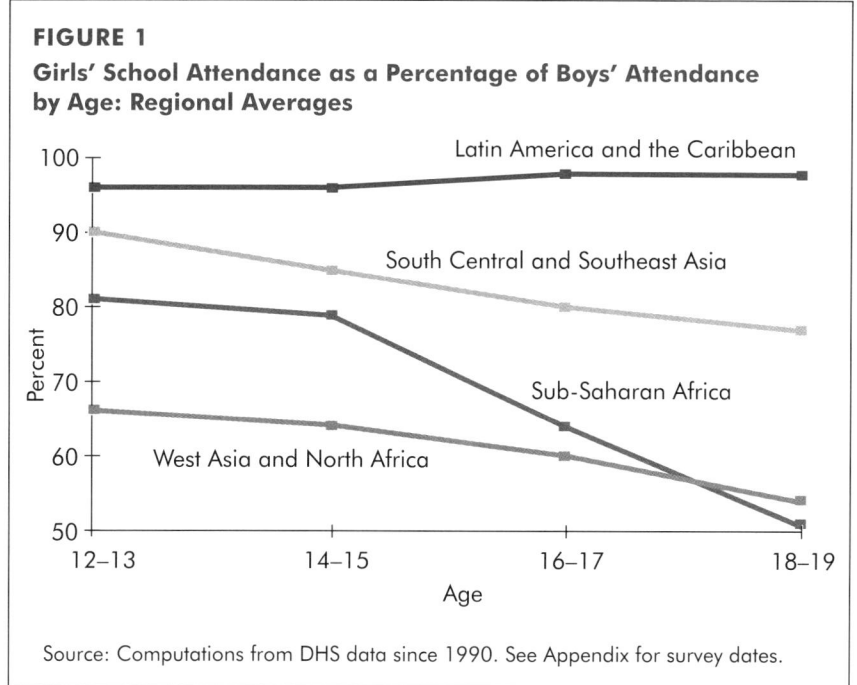

FIGURE 1

Girls' School Attendance as a Percentage of Boys' Attendance by Age: Regional Averages

Source: Computations from DHS data since 1990. See Appendix for survey dates.

attendance is 96 percent of boys'), but is somewhat greater among 16–17-year-olds (girls' attendance is 86 percent of boys').

While DHS surveys provide useful data on school attendance and attainment, they offer virtually no information about adolescents' schooling experience—although this situation is slated to change.[10] Full educational histories have not been collected in these surveys. Questions have been confined to current school status and level of schooling achieved. There are no data on age of entry into school, regularity of attendance, reasons for nonattendance, academic performance, experiences in school, school facilities, and attitudes and expectations concerning educational attainment. Even targeted youth surveys usually lack detailed information on school attendance—despite the documented impact of education, through a variety of routes, on reproductive behavior and child survival (Jejeebhoy 1995; Schultz 1993), and the prominent role that school plays in many adolescents' lives.

Even in the absence of such data, it is widely assumed that one can reach adolescents through programs based in secondary schools. Many

---

[9] Analysis of data from a nationally representative survey of adolescents in Egypt in 1997 does not confirm the pattern observed in the DHS data, for reasons as yet unknown. The Egyptian data indicate that, while a girl is less likely than a boy to be enrolled in school at a young age, if she is enrolled, she has about the same probability as a boy of remaining in school during adolescence (El-Tawila et al. 1998; Ibrahim, Mensch, and El Gibaly 1998).

[10] In "MEASURE DHS+," the new USAID-funded DHS project, the quantity and quality of education data collected in surveys will be enhanced considerably.

adolescent fertility and reproductive health surveys are directed at young people in school (often just at the secondary level) or have a substantial school-based component (Amazigo et al. 1997; Twa-Twa 1997; Youri 1994). This approach is often off the mark. For example, in sub-Saharan African countries where researchers have examined the grade levels of schoolchildren aged 6–14, the majority of school-going 14-year-olds are behind the appropriate grade level for their age as a result of late school-entry and grade repetition. Moreover, the proportion of adolescents who fall behind grade or drop out increases with age, and a nontrivial proportion have never attended school (Lloyd and Blanc 1996). These findings provide indirect evidence that the majority of adolescent girls in the region are not in secondary school. Indeed, a study in Kenya revealed that in Kilifi, a particularly poor district—which is plausibly representative of rural areas in other African countries—43 percent of girls aged 16–18 are in primary school, 17 percent are in secondary school, and the rest are not in school.[11] There is evidence that this phenomenon of adolescents attending primary school also exists in South Asia.[12]

The differential between girls' and boys' school attainment is the result of a variety of governmental and private decisions. Developing countries currently spend an average of nearly 4 percent of gross national product on education, with sub-Saharan Africa spending nearly 6 percent and Asia less than 4 percent (UNESCO 1997). The budgetary process related to education has particular consequences for adolescents, not only with respect to levels of investment per pupil, but also with respect to the composition of school-going youth. Allocations within the education sector between primary, secondary, and tertiary education tend to favor higher education at the expense of primary schooling. In the many settings in which girls' dropout rates increase with schooling level at a far greater rate than boys', this budgetary choice is biased in favor of boys.

The widespread imbalance in access to education in urban, semi-urban, and rural settings also has implications for girls. In Eritrea, for example, 100 percent of the urban population lives within 5 kilometers of a primary school, while this is true of only about one-half of the rural population (National Statistics Office of Eritrea and Macro International 1997). A comparison of rural and urban residents' access to primary school in five countries where the DHS Service Availability Module was

---

[11] See Ajayi et al. (1997) for a discussion of the survey from which these data are drawn.

[12] In the rural district of Bangladesh where Amin is conducting research, "although children are supposed to enter school at the age of five, in practice they start much later...." This has led to "a high proportion of girls aged 13–19 ... in primary school when in fact they are of secondary school age" (Amin 1996: 192).

administered—Colombia, Dominican Republic, Ecuador, Tunisia, and Zimbabwe—shows a similar, although attenuated pattern (Wilkinson, Njogu, and Abderrahim 1993).[13]

In places where parents do not want girls exposed to boys and men, not only in the classroom, but also on the way to and from school, the distance between a girl's residence and school may be a pivotal determinant of her school attendance (Khan 1993). In Pakistan, where schools are sex segregated even at the primary level, 21 percent of girls in rural areas do not have a school within one kilometer of their residence; this is true of only 9 percent of boys in these areas. A recent study in Pakistan found measurable differences in parents' willingness to send daughters to school based on the distance between home and school; this factor did not enter into parents' deliberations about sending sons to school (Sathar and Lloyd 1994).

In sub-Saharan Africa, where (as noted above) girls' school enrollment declines steeply during adolescence, family resistance to girls' schooling may be founded on a fear that girls will fall prey to sexual harassment in, or on the way to and from, school. A recent study in Kenya found that girls' progress in the classroom is often undermined by teachers' attitudes and by teasing on the part of male classmates (Mensch and Lloyd 1998). Further analysis of the data from this study revealed that dropout rates for girls were higher in schools that discriminate in favor of boys or against girls (Lloyd, Mensch, and Clark 1998).[14]

Many governments pass on the cost of education to parents in the form of fees, even at the primary school level. While household expenditure data in developing countries are limited, there is evidence that 5–10 percent of household consumption is devoted to education, on average, with the poorest families expending up to 20 percent (Herz et al. 1991). School fees—which may include the cost of tuition, uniforms, and textbooks—may impede girls' school attendance in cases where parents feel they cannot afford to educate all of their children. In parts of sub-Saharan Africa, school fees may force some girls to acquire "sugar dad-

---

[13] The DHS Service Availability Module was designed to assess the presence of family planning and health services in sampling clusters in which the survey was administered. In addition to the data on family planning and health, data were collected on schools and other service sites, such as post offices and markets. For five of the 11 countries included in the service availability report published by the DHS (the five listed in the text), this information was collected in urban as well as rural clusters.

[14] "[S]chool environments where boys are favored in class and provided with a more supportive environment in terms of advice, where teachers take the importance of hard subjects like Math less seriously for girls than for boys, where boys are left free to harass girls and where girls' experience of less equal treatment is not fully recognized by boys are discouraging to girls" (Lloyd, Mensch, and Clark 1998: 21).

dies"—older men who provide tuition in exchange for sexual favors (Bledsoe 1990; Odaga and Heneveld 1995; Oppong 1995).

Parents' perceptions of the indirect opportunity costs of educating children are often unfavorable to girls' school attendance (Herz et al. 1991; Hill and King 1993). Because girls' labor is valued at home, parents may withdraw their daughters from school or never send them in the first place. As noted earlier, domestic responsibilities do not always prevent girls from going to school, but girls in school generally bear a double burden of school and household work, according to the few existing studies in this area (see "Domestic roles and responsibilities").[15]

Parents' dim view of girls' earning power may be another deterrent to their school attendance (Herz et al. 1991). Yet, according to the World Bank's former chief economist, every year of schooling increases a girl's individual earning power by 10–20 percent (Summers 1992). Parents who recognize the economic benefits of educating a daughter may, nevertheless, believe that these gains will be realized by the girl's marital, not natal, family (Greene 1997).

Even when parents send their daughters to school, their rationale for doing so may reflect underlying views of appropriate gender roles. Among the Annany in Nigeria, formal education is thought to enhance a girl's value in marriage by increasing her familiarity with health care services and the other requirements of running a household (Osom 1989). In Egypt, educating girls is justified by many families as a way to make their daughters into better wives and mothers. The reasoning, according to a headmistress, is that an educated girl knows: "How to act as a female. How to become a housewife. How to become a wife. How to treat her husband, how to raise her children . . ." (Herrera 1992: 28).

In sum, supply-side decisions regarding education budgets, school fees, locations of schools, teacher training, curriculum, and so forth often interact with demand-side factors—namely, community attitudes, parental fears, and discriminatory income-allocation patterns within families—in ways that are unfavorable to girls' education. Compared to boys, girls in developing countries outside Latin America and the Caribbean and the Philippines are widely deprived of secondary educa-

---

[15] Interestingly, one of the few studies that examine the impact of household work on adolescent school attendance is based on data from Peru, a country with near gender equity in school attendance (although this may not have been the case when the survey was fielded). The study, based on the 1985–86 Peru Living Standards Survey, ignores boys altogether, despite the fact that data on schooling, labor market activity, and domestic work are available for all members of the household. If domestic work is, in fact, a deterrent to girls' school attendance, then one might ask: what is deterring boys' attendance at nearly an equal rate? (Levison and Moe 1997).

tion, and even primary education in some countries, particularly in the poorest communities.[16]

Raising girls' levels of schooling, even by a few years, has widely documented benefits. Women's education is associated with better health and nutrition, increased child survival, later age at marriage, and lower fertility (Jejeebhoy 1995; LeVine 1982; Subbarao and Raney 1993).[17] Education increases girls' knowledge of and exposure to the outside world; indeed, in the absence of schooling, girls in many societies have no interaction with the world beyond the family.[18] Education strengthens girls' decisionmaking power within the family, promotes their social and physical mobility, and increases their economic independence and control over resources, all of which enhance their autonomy (Jejeebhoy 1995). Educated girls become educated mothers with increased livelihood prospects; they also have a greater propensity than similarly educated males to invest in children's schooling, and often give special attention to daughters' education. Thus, the benefits of female education are passed on to the next generation (Herz and Khandker 1991).

Thoughtful investment in the education sector is arguably the most powerful governmental instrument for improving the lives of adolescent girls.[19] At the same time, convincing parents and communities of the value of investing in their daughters' education, and creating incentives for them to do so, are essential. The viability of such financial incentive schemes was demonstrated in Bangladesh, where a secondary-school

> **Thoughtful investment in the education sector is arguably the most powerful governmental instrument for improving the lives of adolescent girls.**

---

[16] One explanation that has been given for why Latin American and Caribbean girls are not educationally disadvantaged compared to their counterparts in other regions is that the Christian missionary tradition "constricted women's freedom less than have Moslem or Confucian influences" in other societies (Bustillo 1993: 176). It is further hypothesized that indigenous Indian cultures in Latin America and the Caribbean were quite egalitarian (Bustillo 1993). Income undoubtedly plays a role as well: wealthier countries can afford the "luxury" of educating women.

[17] While the vast majority of studies that examine the association between female schooling and fertility find an overall negative correlation, there is a debate in the literature about whether fertility is higher among women with a couple of years of schooling compared to those with no schooling, particularly in sub-Saharan Africa (Jejeebhoy 1995). The argument in favor of this contention is that women with one or two years of education breastfeed their children for shorter periods or avoid it altogether, and reduce the length of postpartum abstinence, but do not reduce their desired family size. However, Ainsworth, Beegle, and Nyamete (1996) argue that, since literacy is rarely conferred with one or two years of schooling in developing countries, a sample selectivity explanation may be more plausible: females who leave school early may be the least capable academically or may come from families committed to early marriage and childbearing.

[18] While "young adult men are exposed to new ideas through their wider contacts with the world outside family and local community . . . for [women] formal schooling remains perhaps the primary channel for the transmission of new ideas" (Jejeebhoy 1995: 36).

[19] Knodel and Jones argue that the prominence given to gender inequality in schooling in the Programme of Action of the 1994 International Conference on Population

Formal policy concern with adolescent work has been centered for most of this century on the contentious subject of child labor.

scholarship program for girls markedly increased their school enrollment (Amin and Sedgh 1998).

While all children benefit from schooling, the advantages that education bestows on girls are likely to be much broader in scope and intergenerational reach than those bestowed on boys. International charters and declarations acknowledge that increasing education levels, particularly among females, is essential to social, economic, and human development; furthermore, they affirm that education is a fundamental human right. Girls' lesser access to education is an injustice for girls as individuals, and it carries serious consequences for society.

Work

Formal policy concern with adolescent work has been centered for most of this century on the contentious subject of child labor. In 1919, an international convention established 14 as the minimum age at which children could be employed. In 1973, this age was raised to 15; that same year, an International Labour Office (ILO) convention recommended that it be increased to 16 (UNICEF 1997). The 1989 Convention on the Rights of the Child provides the most comprehensive policy guidance on the subject; in Article 32, it recognizes the right of children (up to age 18) to be protected from work that threatens their health, education, or development.

Despite good intentions to protect children from harmful labor, in reality many children do work, often beginning at an early age. Assessing the extent and nature of girls' work is difficult, however, for several reasons. Definitions of work and employment, particularly for females, are in transition. Time-use data illuminating girls' work contribution are highly limited. Gender biases in the reporting of work affect researchers and adolescent respondents alike. Country comparisons of girls' and women's labor force participation are problematic because of major inconsistencies in the definition of work. Girls and women in

---

and Development ignores the socioeconomic inequality that is "nearly universal" and "more pronounced" (1996: 812). They state that the gender gap in schooling is large only in southern Asian and Arab countries and that in sub-Saharan Africa the issue of primary concern is low enrollment among all children. Because their argument is based on an analysis of aggregate enrollment ratios, they miss the point that while gender gaps in school attendance may be small among younger children, they expand during adolescence, particularly in sub-Saharan Africa. Knodel and Jones also note that fertility has fallen in countries that have not closed the gender gap in secondary education (e.g., Bangladesh) and has failed to decline in countries where female school enrollment exceeds male enrollment (e.g., the Philippines). Underlying their critique is the view that education is important primarily because of its links to lower fertility. They ignore the larger issue that education is the main instrument for improving girls' and women's status. As we and others argue, girls' education has multiple benefits, only one of which is reduced family size.

developing countries often work outside the modern sector and without clear remuneration, with the result that levels of productive female work are often underestimated (Amin and Lloyd forthcoming; Dixon-Mueller 1985; Lloyd 1991).

The ILO estimates that a minimum of 73 million 10–14-year-olds—the equivalent of 13 percent of children of this age in the developing world—are working for income. This estimate is based on results from child labor surveys (UNICEF 1997). Because of the difficulty of determining who is working, other approaches to obtaining information about children's work have been suggested, such as ascertaining how many children are not in school. A 1991 UNICEF report titled "Children and Women in India" (based on data from the 1981 census) estimated that of the 140 million children aged 6–14 in that country, approximately 75 million were out of school. The report asserted that "most of the children of school age who are not in school may be expected to be in some sort of work . . ." (cited in Burra 1997: 14). Burra questions these data and the dubious deductive processes underlying their interpretation, and suggests that a better way to estimate the extent of child labor is to examine work places and industries where children are likely to be concentrated. Her own inquiry in India turned up concentrations of girls in specific industries, such as the *beedi* (local cigarette) and food-processing-industries, and home-based industries such as incense making, *papad* (an Indian savory) preparation, the making of paper bags, gem polishing, and the sub-assembly of electronic items (Burra 1997).

To our knowledge, no labor force surveys have focused exclusively on adolescents. The limited cross-country data on adolescents' work status presented in this section are drawn from ILO statistics and DHS data, although the latter are only available for older adolescents. The ILO collects data on the "economically active" population, defined as persons "who furnish the supply of labour for the production of goods and services during a specified time-reference period" (ILO 1996: 5). The ILO strongly cautions that differences in the definition of economic activity from country to country make comparisons problematic. It specifically notes that women's activity rates are often not comparable between countries because women frequently work without pay for family enterprises and countries differ in the degree to which such workers are included in official data; for example, some countries only include family workers who are employed for more than one-third of a standard working day. The ILO also notes that activity rates among young people should be "compared with caution," not only because of the phenomenon of family employment, but also because of differences in counting "unemployed persons not previously employed, and . . . students engaged in part-time economic activities" (ILO 1996: 5–6). Table 4 presents ILO economic activity rates for adolescents in countries that supplied such data. Perhaps the main finding to note is that reported rates are much higher for boys than for girls. With the exception of Burkina Faso (the only sub-Saharan African country with available data), there is no country in which at least half of girls are reported to be economically active, whereas in 8 of the 18 countries more than 50 percent of boys aged 15–19 are reported to be in this category.

In the DHS, respondents are asked whether they currently have jobs, in addition to housework, for which they are paid in cash or kind;[20] the interpretation of "current" is left up to the respondent (Amin and Lloyd forthcoming). Figures 2 and 3 present data on current activity of adolescent girls by marital status. Figure 2 indicates that work, as defined by the DHS, does not figure prominently in the lives of unmarried girls. In 20 of the 32 countries, unmarried girls who are out of school are more likely to report not being engaged in any formal, remunerated activity than they are likely to report working. In 10 of these countries, a "mystery" concerning girls' adolescent experience emerges when over one-third of unmarried girls are reported to be neither in school nor working. How are we to interpret these statistics? Could they mean that unmarried girls underreport working because they believe that they are not "supposed" to be working or seeking work? Or that many girls are doing unpaid domestic work, which does not fit the DHS definition of work? Or that girls, especially those from wealthier families, have considerable free time? In the absence of definitive time-use data, which would enable us to investigate how girls occupy themselves and how this activity varies by social class, income, and residence, we have no certain answers.

What we do learn from the DHS data is that there is considerable variability in unmarried girls' work experience. While the majority of unmarried adolescent girls who are not in school are not working, a non-trivial fraction of their counterparts in Latin America and sub-Saharan Africa who attend school also work. In 7 of 8 Latin American countries and 11 of 20 sub-Saharan African countries in Figure 2, more than 10 percent of girls in school also report working.

The work status of married adolescent girls also needs further clarification. While the majority of these DHS respondents in 28 out of 38

---

[20] To determine their work status, respondents are asked: "Aside from your own housework, are you currently working?" Those who answer "no" are then asked: "As you know, some women take up jobs for which they are paid in cash or kind. Others sell things, have a small business or work on the family farm or in the family business. Are you currently doing any of these things or any other work?"

TABLE 4
Percentage of Adolescents Who Are Economically Active

Region/Country	Age	Girls	Boys
Latin America and the Caribbean			
Belize[1]	14–19	18.9	47.9
Brazil[2]	10–14	14.9	28.1
	15–19*	45.4	72.2
Chile[1]	15–19**	12.6	25.7
El Salvador[2]	10–14	6.1	19.3
	15–19	23.3	57.8
Guyana[1]	15–19	27.3	54.2
Honduras[1]	10–14	4.8	17.8
	15–19**	22.4	67.0
Jamaica[1]	14–19	23.5	32.3
Mexico[1]	10–14	6.8	15.7
	15–19	29.6	60.4
Panama[1]	15–19	22.6	45.9
Peru[2]	15–19	23.1	43.9
Trinidad-Tobago[1]	15–19	21.2	39.4
South Central and Southeast Asia			
Indonesia[1]	10–14	7.9	10.5
	15–19	35.0	43.1
Pakistan[1]	10–14	6.9	16.8
	15–19**	12.1	52.3
Philippines[2]	15–19***	28.1	46.5
Sri Lanka[1]	10–14	0.5	1.1
	15–19	18.2	28.5
Sub-Saharan Africa			
Burkina Faso[1]	10–14	61.0	63.9
	15–19	72.4	79.3
West Asia and North Africa			
Egypt[1]	15–19**	11.3	35.4
Turkey[1]	12–14	17.4	21.9
	15–19**	33.9	52.6

* Excludes institutional households and members of the armed forces living in barracks.
** Excludes members of the armed forces.
*** Includes members of the armed forces living in private households.

[1] Derived from ILO Labor Force Survey.
[2] Derived from ILO Household Survey.

Note: The International Labour Office defines "economically active" persons as those "who furnish the supply of labour for the production of goods and services" (ILO 1996: 5).

Source: International Labour Office (1996).

countries report not working, there are clear regional differences, as shown in Figure 3. In Muslim countries in Asia and North Africa—Bangladesh, Pakistan, Egypt, Morocco, Turkey, and Yemen—over one-quarter of married 15–19-year-old girls are classified as not working, not in school, having no children, and not being pregnant; approximately one-quarter of married 15–19-year-old girls are classified as not working

FIGURE 2
Current Activity of Never-Married Girls Aged 15–19

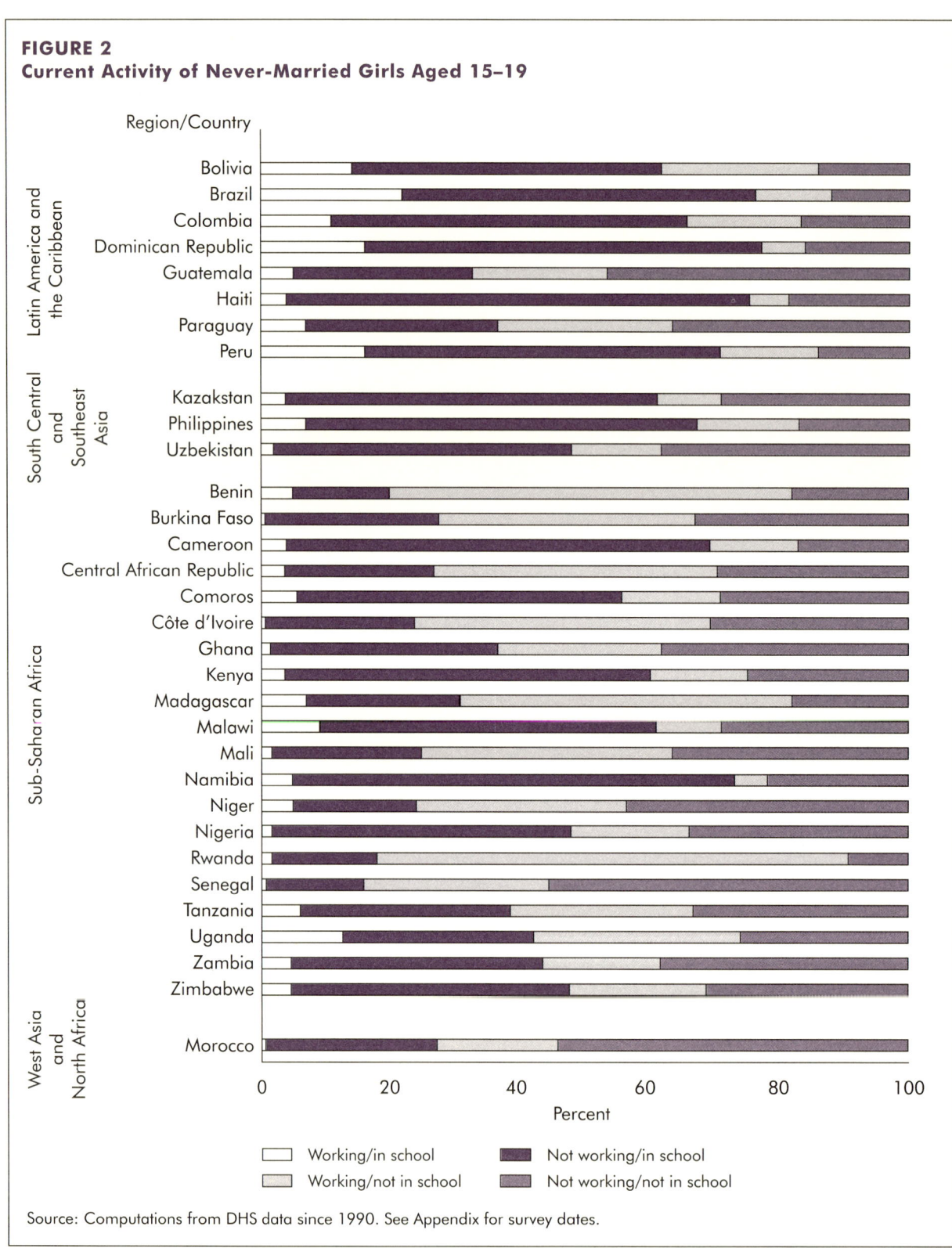

Source: Computations from DHS data since 1990. See Appendix for survey dates.

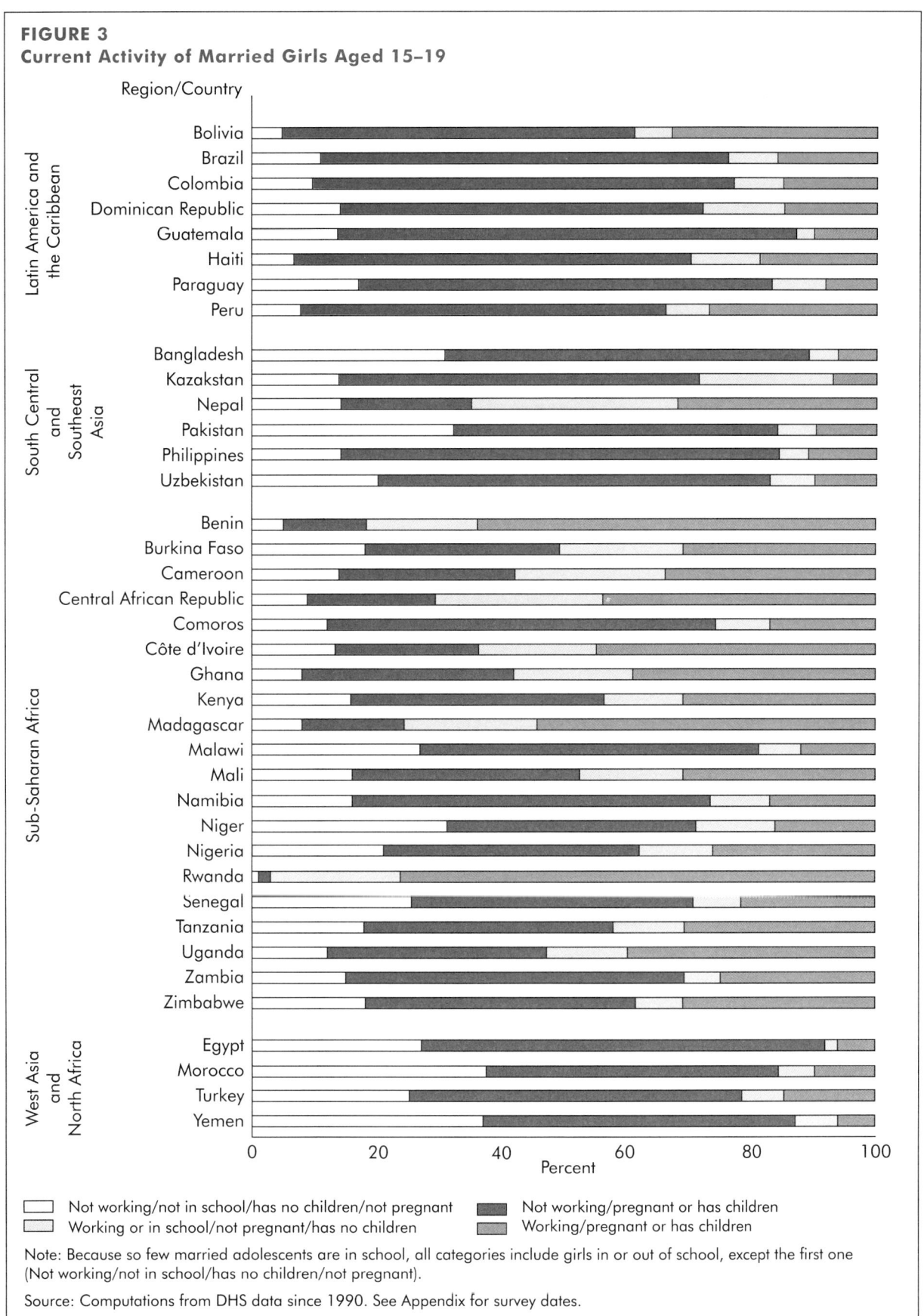

FIGURE 3
Current Activity of Married Girls Aged 15–19

Region/Country

Latin America and the Caribbean
- Bolivia
- Brazil
- Colombia
- Dominican Republic
- Guatemala
- Haiti
- Paraguay
- Peru

South Central and Southeast Asia
- Bangladesh
- Kazakstan
- Nepal
- Pakistan
- Philippines
- Uzbekistan

Sub-Saharan Africa
- Benin
- Burkina Faso
- Cameroon
- Central African Republic
- Comoros
- Côte d'Ivoire
- Ghana
- Kenya
- Madagascar
- Malawi
- Mali
- Namibia
- Niger
- Nigeria
- Rwanda
- Senegal
- Tanzania
- Uganda
- Zambia
- Zimbabwe

West Asia and North Africa
- Egypt
- Morocco
- Turkey
- Yemen

Percent — 0 20 40 60 80 100

☐ Not working/not in school/has no children/not pregnant   ■ Not working/pregnant or has children

▨ Working or in school/not pregnant/has no children   ▨ Working/pregnant or has children

Note: Because so few married adolescents are in school, all categories include girls in or out of school, except the first one (Not working/not in school/has no children/not pregnant).

Source: Computations from DHS data since 1990. See Appendix for survey dates.

and having children or being pregnant. While a greater proportion of married girls of this age report working in Latin America and the Philippines than in other countries in Asia and in North Africa, in all countries of these three regions well over half (56–77 percent) of married 15–19-year-olds report not working and having children or being pregnant. This pattern contrasts with sub-Saharan Africa: in only 4 of 20 countries in Figure 3 do more than 50 percent of married adolescent girls report being at home with children; on average, 48 percent of married girls with children report working.

This sketch of married and unmarried adolescent girls' employment, drawn from the formal data, is supplemented by information from time-use studies, ethnographic observations, and a new wave of schooling studies. This research confirms that the burden of home-based work falls disproportionately on adolescent girls (see "Domestic roles and responsibilities"). The few existing time-use studies further reveal that females' *overall* workload is greater than males'. Indeed, a recent analysis and review of the literature finds that "women's workday is longer than that of men in 15 of 17 studies" (Brown and Haddad 1995: 10). While time-use studies have rarely investigated thoroughly how adolescents occupy themselves,[21] they generally reinforce the picture presented in the ethnographic literature. For example, a rural labor force survey in Kenya, which included approximately 8,000 households, found that girls aged 8–14 worked an average of 19 hours per week, while boys of that age averaged 14 hours.[22] The differential in work hours was greater for older adolescents: 32 hours per week for girls aged 15–19, versus 18 hours for boys of that age (derived from Figure 4 in Sebstad 1991).

There are a few settings in which girls' overall workload does not exceed boys'; but even in these rare cases, the nature of girls' and boys' work differs. In the Philippines, a time-use study reports that boys and girls spend the same amount of time working; nevertheless, there is a "strong division of labor along gender lines" (Bouis et al. 1994: 67). In Bangladesh, an observation study of 351 children aged 6–19 found that boys' and girls' contributions to productive activity were equal; however,

---

[21] For example, only three broad age categories were used in a seven-country comparative analysis of gender differences in time allocation: children 13 and under, adults 14–50, and adults over 50 (Brown and Haddad 1995). To the extent that data are collected on time use prior to adulthood, the emphasis is usually on child labor among those under age 15—the minimum age for work set by the ILO (see, for example, UNICEF 1997).

[22] Work was defined to include domestic chores, fetching water, collecting firewood, unpaid family labor, wage employment, self-employment, and nonfarm business.

girls' productive work was confined to the household sphere while boys' work consisted almost exclusively of income-generating labor.[23]

While the extent of girls' work outside the home varies from region to region, girls generally have fewer opportunities than boys to work for wages (though such opportunities are scarce for adolescents of both sexes in most places). The Kenyan survey cited above indicates that rural females are much less likely than males to be compensated in cash for their work (6 percent versus 37 percent of 15–64-year-olds) (Sebstad 1991). The Bangladesh observation study cited above showed that girls spend less than half as much time on income-earning work as boys, whether or not they are in school. Girls aged 13–19 who reported any school attendance over the 12-month period of data collection—and nearly half did (49 percent)—devoted an average of 1.7 hours a day to income-generating work, while those out of school averaged 2.3 hours; boys of the same age who attended school (53 percent) devoted 3.5 hours a day to income-generating work, while those out of school averaged 7 hours (Arends-Kuenning, Sedgh, and Amin 1998).[24]

Many adolescent girls are engaged in two domains of work that have been largely invisible to official eyes: domestic service and commercial sex. We discuss these two categories of work below, before turning to a discussion of the benefits of legitimate income-earning work for adolescent girls.

Exploitative work: domestic service and commercial sex

Domestic service is possibly the largest "employer" of adolescent girls. The aforementioned ILO estimate of 73 million working children aged 10–14 would increase considerably if it included children in domestic service, the vast majority of whom are probably girls (UNICEF 1997). Domestic work is increasingly viewed as being undervalued, whether it is rendered in the worker's residence or elsewhere. Attempts are being made at the national and international policy levels to give domestic work economic standing and to regulate the participation of children and adults in this work.

Poor, rural families and recent migrants to urban areas are the most likely families to place their girls in domestic service (Chaney and Castro

> Many adolescent girls are engaged in two domains of work that have been largely invisible to official eyes: domestic service and commercial sex.

---

[23] An activity was considered productive if it directly generated cash. Thus, housework, the storing of cereal and rice for family consumption, and vegetable gardening were not counted as productive work, while vegetable marketing and the making of handicrafts and sweets for sale were counted as such (Amin 1998).

[24] Data are drawn from Amin's 1995–96 survey titled "Family Structure and Change in Rural Bangladesh."

Concerns about child labor and exploitation have generated a negative attitude toward girls' work.

1989). These families may reason that an absent adolescent girl is not only one less mouth to feed, but is also a potential source of income for the family.

The conditions of domestic work are often grim. Domestic servants generally have no set hours of work, are given very little free time, and are often prevented from leaving the house. Young domestics may be at risk of sexual abuse by employers and members of employers' families. A study in Peru of 100 families that employed domestics found that 60 percent of the adolescent males in these households had their first sexual experience with a "house girl" (Barker and Knaul 1992).

UNICEF takes a strong position that the participation of young and adolescent girls in domestic service is not an unavoidable cultural choice, nor is it the prerogative of parents to conscript their daughters into this service. Rather, they state, this work "should be acknowledged for what it has become: the exploitation of child labor" (UNICEF 1997: 30).

The involvement of adolescent girls (and boys, to some extent) in commercial sex work is the most egregious form of exploitative child labor. This problem has generated the greatest publicity in Southeast Asia. UNICEF estimates that there are 80,000 prostitutes younger than age 18 in Thailand alone (Chantrakar 1994). One study reports that nearly three-quarters of Burmese prostitutes in Thailand are in their late teens and early 20s (Pyne 1992). Among bar workers in the Philippines, a recent study found that 20 percent of some 500,000 prostitutes were girls younger than 17 (Barker and Knaul 1992; Bagasao 1992).

The decision that a girl will have sexual relations is often not made by the girl but by her family. Throughout Southeast Asia, national campaigns condemn the practice of selling girls into prostitution and caution parents and communities not to send their girls to cities for ill-defined work.

Employment in the commercial sex trade not only violates a girl's childhood and human dignity, it often destroys her health and may end her life. This is increasingly being recognized by policymakers: a World Congress Against Commercial Sexual Exploitation of Children was held for the first time in 1996 (UNICEF 1997).

Benefits of work for adolescent girls

Concerns about child labor and exploitation have generated a negative attitude toward girls' work and have even inadvertently created some bad outcomes for girls. Efforts to improve working conditions for boys and girls in regulated industries may actually force children into more hazardous employment. A recent study in Bangladesh tracked children after they were dismissed from modern-sector, albeit illegal, jobs; many of these children were found to be working in dangerous situations, in workshops where they were paid less, or as prostitutes (UNICEF 1997).

Inspections of work environments in free-trade zones have often revealed disgraceful conditions. Yet, too little attention has been given to the question: "Compared to *what?*" For many adolescent girls, wage-earning work (under the right circumstances) could represent a step up in the working world. Moreover, girls' increasing participation in wage-earning work appears to be inevitable. In every region except sub-Saharan Africa, female labor force participation has increased since 1970 (United Nations 1995).

Girls may have more time available for income-earning work as economic modernization reduces some of the demands on their time. Comparing time-use data from the same Bangladeshi villages in 1976 and 1994, Amin and colleagues discovered that the work hours of both adolescent girls and older women had declined considerably, "mainly as a result of the mechanization of post-harvest labor, which was traditionally performed by women" (Amin et al. 1998: 186).[25]

Greater time availability; the need for paid work; girls' rising expectations; the "feminization" of the export-oriented textile industry in parts of Asia, as well as in Costa Rica and Mauritius (Anker 1998); and corporations' quest for cheap labor may explain girls' rapid entry into factory work in some countries.[26] In the late 1970s, there were about four factories in the garment industry in Bangladesh; in 1995 there were 2,400 factories employing 1.2 million people. Of these workers, 90 percent were female—a large share of them adolescents. Unmarried girls employed in these garment factories may endure onerous work conditions, but they also experience pride in their earnings, maintain a higher standard of dress than their unemployed counterparts, and, most significantly,

---

[25] While girls' time availability may be increasing on average, considerable heterogeneity remains among individual girls, even in poor communities. A baseline study in Maqattam, Egypt indicated that the time-use profiles of girls from equally poor families varied considerably, depending on the nature of the family enterprise (Assaad and Bruce 1997).

[26] Anker reports this trend in Costa Rica, Hong Kong, Mauritius, and Fiji in the 1970s and early 1980s. Data are apparently not available for more recent years; however, this trend appears to have continued into the 1990s and exists in other countries—Bangladesh, for example (Amin et al. 1998). Anker does not break down his analysis by age; but Wolf, who has studied female factory workers in Java, reports that most females in the industrial work force are young and unmarried—a phenomenon that she says is "typical . . . of other Third World countries." She notes that "researchers have pointed to the role of the state in proliferating gender stereotypes of docile, 'nimble-fingered' Asian females in order to draw foreign investors to Southeast Asia" (Wolf 1992: 115–116).

develop an identity apart from being a child or wife. Although the majority of these girls, particularly those aged 10–14, turn most of their earnings over to their families (sometimes for their dowries), older girls retain a greater portion of their income—only 48 percent of those aged 15–19 pool their income with their families'—and thereby gain some economic independence (Amin et al. 1998).

One of the most impressive social effects of garment-factory work has been delayed marriage. Only 8 percent of 15–19-year-old garment workers, and 19 percent of 20–24 year-old workers, had married by age 15. By contrast, 40 and 38 percent (respectively) of same-aged girls had married by age 15 in villages that send girls to garment factories; in villages that do not send girls to do this work, the comparable figures were 58 and 55 percent (Amin et al. 1998). The lower rate of early marriage among nonworkers in villages that send girls to garment factories, compared to villages that do not, indicates that girls' employment may transform social norms not only for working girls, but also for their non-working peers.

This case suggests that legitimate income-generating work could transform the nature of girls' adolescent experience. It could provide them with a degree of autonomy, self-respect, and freedom from traditional gender roles. More importantly, perhaps, it could help to reframe the second decade of girls' lives as a transitional period prior to marriage and childbearing, in which girls have a chance to develop as individuals and gain knowledge and skills to lay the foundation for a more satisfying and productive adulthood.

When the gender dimensions of work are properly appreciated, it is obvious that girls' employment can be classified in two categories: work that is harmful and work that may offer girls some liberating possibilities. International efforts to curb exploitative forms of girls' labor that were previously ignored—such as domestic service rendered under inhumane and unjust conditions and forced participation in commercial sex work—are certainly welcome. At the same time, opportunities and pressure for girls to work must be examined with a more neutral eye.

As policy interest in adolescents (and all youth) builds, so does the need for more studies of current and future labor supply, work conditions, and the meaning of work for girls. A priority for those concerned about the welfare of adolescent girls is to find out more about how income-generating work can be structured to promote an adolescence that is, at the very least, protected and productive.

Chapter 3

Adolescent Reproductive Health, Marriage, and Childbearing

The sexual and reproductive aspects of adolescents' lives have received a good deal more research attention than the contextual factors discussed in the previous chapter. The developing-country literature rarely links reproductive outcomes to social processes other than to note their association with education (see, for example, Singh 1998b); however, as we have stated, our belief is that these outcomes are very much a manifestation of social processes, notably gender dynamics. Thus, we deliberately discuss reproductive health, marriage, and childbearing after having analyzed the social and economic context of adolescent girls' lives.

In the sections below, we examine aspects of adolescents' health status; girls' experience of menstruation; adolescent sexual activity; knowledge of reproductive biology and health; fertility regulation; marriage; and childbearing, both within and outside marriage. As in the previous chapter, we draw on data from the DHS and other surveys, where available, and indicate areas in which data are notably scarce.

Health status

It is worth commenting on the general health status of adolescents before we consider their reproductive health and behavior. While mortality rates are lower during adolescence than at any other time of life (Coale and Demeny 1983), some diseases affect young people disproportionately and/or are more aggressive during adolescence, such as schistosomiasis and other intestinal parasites and tuberculosis.[1] Moreover, certain behaviors that are typically initiated during adolescence—name-

---

[1] See WHO and UNICEF (1995) for a review and annotated bibliography of literature on the health of young people.

ly the use of alcohol, tobacco, and other drugs—often have serious health consequences, either immediately or later in life (Senderowitz 1995).

The greatest nutritional problem facing adolescents appears to be anemia. In four of six developing countries included in a series of case studies of anemia, recently undertaken by the International Center for Research on Women (ICRW),[2] the prevalence of anemia among adolescents was around one-third or higher. Anemia was as common among boys as among girls, indicating that both sexes have high iron requirements for rapid physical development during adolescence.[3] As this growth slackens in later adolescence, the prevalence of anemia in boys appears to decline relative to girls, who continue to lose iron during menstruation. According to a World Health Organization (WHO) report on the health of young people, "anemia is twice as frequent in adolescent and adult women as in men" (WHO 1993: 13).[4]

Undernutrition was also observed among adolescent boys and girls in several of the countries included in the ICRW studies, notably Benin, India, and Nepal, where one-quarter to one-half of adolescents were below the fifth percentile on the National Center for Health Statistics/WHO body mass index (weight/height[2]). As with anemia, undernutrition was common among boys and girls; indeed, two times as many boys as girls had a low body mass index in seven of the eight countries where undernutrition in both sexes was studied. The literature on sex differentials in nutritional status is inconsistent, however. According to the WHO report, "girls and young women are more likely to be malnourished than boys and young men" (WHO 1993: 15).[5] It is not clear whether this assertion is based on epidemiological studies or on an assumption that adolescent girls are disadvantaged in this area, as they are in many other domains of their lives. The ICRW report states that "the disproportionate number of boys suffering from under-nutrition was a surprise" (Kurz and Johnson-Welch 1994: 10).[6]

In females, anemia can increase the risk of negative reproductive outcomes, such as miscarriage, stillbirth, premature birth, low birth-

---

[2] For an overview of these case studies, see Kurz and Johnson-Welch (1994).

[3] This finding confirms earlier research by nutritionists.

[4] It is noteworthy that adolescent boys are not mentioned, implying that boys are not as likely to be anemic. This contradicts the findings of the ICRW studies, as well as earlier research cited in the ICRW report.

[5] The ICRW and WHO reports may disagree because they consider different indicators of undernourishment. It is not possible to determine this, however, because the WHO report is not sufficiently technical.

[6] The researchers postulate that two factors may contribute to this phenomenon: the differential in male and female maturation rates; and the likelihood that anemia impedes weight gain in boys more than in girls because boys gain more muscle during adolescence and, therefore, need greater stores of iron.

weight, perinatal mortality, and maternal mortality (Kurz and Johnson-Welch 1994). The consequences of adolescent undernutrition on reproductive health have not been thoroughly investigated; however, stunting, an indicator of poor nutrition, is known to be associated with obstructed labor as a result of cephalo-pelvic disproportion—a problem for younger adolescent girls whose pelvis has not yet reached adult size (WHO and UNICEF 1995). There is some evidence that poor nutrition has a negative impact on children's school attendance and attainment (Kurz and Johnson-Welch 1994); these educational outcomes have ramifying effects on girls' wellbeing, reproductive and otherwise (see "Schooling" in Chapter 2).

The extent of reproductive health problems among adolescents is a matter of increasing concern, but also a matter of debate. Cultural obstacles to open inquiry into the sexual lives of unmarried and married adolescents impede researchers' ability to collect data in this area; moreover, clinical assessments are costly and seldom undertaken on large populations. Thus, estimates of the prevalence of reproductive health problems among adolescents vary, sometimes widely. Prevalence data on sexually transmitted diseases (STDs) are rare, particularly in population-based samples, and data broken down by age groups are even rarer. According to a recent review of the epidemiological data, when STD levels for girls are reported by age, rates are highest among 15–24-year-olds; however, most of these data are collected from family planning and antenatal clinics (Wasserheit and Holmes 1992), and girls who attend such clinics are unlikely to be representative of sexually active adolescents.

Given that a large proportion of older adolescents in developing countries are sexually active, either within or outside marriage; and given the likely increase in premarital sexual activity (see "Sexual activity") and the spreading epidemics of STDs in these countries, reproductive health problems undoubtedly will be a significant—and, in some cases, mounting—presence in the adolescent population. Indeed, according to two reproductive health experts, "the most recent epidemiological data from surveys, clinical studies, and serologic investigations in the developing world suggest that the STD epidemic [among] adolescents is enlarging globally" (Cates and McPheeters 1997).

For biological and social reasons, adolescent girls are vulnerable to more reproductive health problems than boys—consider their risk of pregnancy-related morbidity and mortality—and (in some places, at least) are more vulnerable to certain problems that affect both sexes, such as HIV infection. To illustrate, two population-based surveys in areas of Tanzania and Uganda revealed that 13–17 percent of females

For biological and social reasons, adolescent girls are vulnerable to more reproductive health problems than boys.

**At the onset of
menstruation,
girls' lives often
change abruptly.**

aged 15–24 were HIV-positive, compared to only 5 percent of males in the same age group (Borongo et al. 1992; Nunn et al. 1994).

Menstruation

Although menarche is but one part of the maturation process, it is often culturally defined as the indicator of girls' maturity and readiness for marriage and sexual activity. While there has been considerable research on the timing of menarche, there is a surprising paucity of research on its social significance, and relatively few studies on natural variability in menstrual cycle characteristics and menstrual dysfunction (Harlow 1995).

At the onset of menstruation, girls' lives often change abruptly. Menstruating females in places as far apart as Papua New Guinea (Herdt 1982) and South India (Ullrich 1977) are required to avoid contact with others. Their activity may be restricted in many domains, including food preparation and consumption, socializing, religious practice, bathing, mobility, school attendance, and sexual activity (Abdalla 1982; Appfel-Marglin 1996; Romero 1988; Shweder 1995).[7] In South India, a girl who has reached menarche is usually prevented from doing field work, especially paid work for other households, which is critical for the lower castes; this activity cannot be resumed until after marriage, when there is no longer a danger of premarital pregnancy (Caldwell, Reddy, and Caldwell 1983). A study in Cuernavaca found that lower-middle-class girls are kept under constant supervision and may be withdrawn from school when they begin to menstruate because they are thought to face an immediate sexual threat from men (Levine 1993). A study in South India reported that one-half of girls who were in school at first menses were withdrawn at that time, "usually to be married as soon as possible, either because menarche is taken as a sign that marriage should be arranged or because of the disgrace and danger of an unmarried pubescent girl being in public" (Caldwell, Reddy, and Caldwell 1985: 41). A small study in rural Egypt found that when girls begin to menstruate, they are prohibited from talking to boys and their daily activity changes—notably, they do less field work. Despite these restrictions, all 41 women in the study were congratulated when they began to bleed because this meant that they were "now ready for marriage and motherhood" (Khattab 1996: 13).

---

[7] Some anthropologists challenge the notion that menstrual taboos are always limiting for females. Buckley and Gottlieb (1988) argue—unconvincingly, we think—that seclusion from men and prohibitions against work are not necessarily considered onerous by girls and women, nor are these restrictions unequivocal evidence of male control or dominance.

In many cultures, menstrual blood is viewed as a "polluting" substance. In southern Africa, according to one anthropological study, the "menstrual blood of women is [believed to be] 'hot' and 'red' and dangerous to men and also to the fertility of cattle and of crops" (Kuper 1982: 19). There is little research on girls' perceptions of menstruation and how these views inhibit or otherwise affect their psychological and social development. Girls' psychological acceptance of menstruation is likely to be undermined when menarche arrives without prior explanation. Although girls may have seen their mothers in seclusion or otherwise observing menstrual taboos, they often do not understand what is happening to them when they begin to bleed. A study of family planning clients in Jamaica found that over one-quarter of them had no information about menstruation at first menses and were often reluctant to tell their mothers or grandmothers for fear of being beaten (Brody 1981). Secluded, restricted, monitored more closely than before menarche, and often lacking much understanding of menstruation, a girl may view her bleeding as a source of shame (Levine 1993; Romero 1988).

The practical and health dimensions of menstruation are almost thoroughly neglected subjects. We know that girls and women use cotton, strips of cloth pinned between their legs, their underpants, or nothing at all to absorb blood flow. Although they may replace and wash these cloths frequently, they may develop low-grade reproductive tract infections (RTIs) if the cloths are not boiled and dried thoroughly before being used again (Wasserheit et al. 1989). This is especially a problem for adolescent girls who are not sexually active and are, thus, unlikely to seek treatment for RTIs. In places where the most extreme forms of female genital mutilation are practiced (e.g., Somalia and parts of Sudan), menstruation is made painful by the tight closing of the labia, which leaves only a small hole through which blood is allowed to flow, increasing risk of infection (Romero 1988).

To manage menstruation, many females, particularly poor ones, in developing countries must make do with materials on hand. In India, girls in Uttar Pradesh use the edge of their saris to absorb blood; in Rajasthan, "adolescent girls are not supposed to wear anything during menstruation and are huddled up in a hut in the village. Abundant sand is considered to act as an absorbent" (Misra 1995: 76). A few local efforts are being made to provide females with better means of managing menstruation. For example, small-scale income-generating projects in Tanzania and Zambia have developed indigenously produced, low-cost, safe materials for this purpose, including sterilized pads (Jiggins 1997).

There is a dearth of information about the sexual and reproductive knowledge of soon-to-be-married partners, the transition to marriage, and the experience of young married couples.

While we know little about girls' menstrual experience, we do know that it has a profound impact on the structure and quality of their lives. Rather than ushering in a protected period of development prior to marriage and childbearing, first menses all too often marks a sudden, sometimes traumatic transition to adult roles and responsibilities and signals a girl's entry into a world in which her value is largely determined by her sexual and reproductive functions.

Sexual activity

Not all adolescent sexual activity has been of equal interest to demographers. Researchers have devoted the bulk of their attention to premarital sex, based on the assumption that sexual activity is increasing among unmarried adolescents. Thus, there is a dearth of information about the sexual and reproductive knowledge of soon-to-be-married partners, the transition to marriage, and the experience of young married couples and their negotiations regarding the intervals between marriage and sexual intercourse and between marriage and first birth. Yet, in many countries, marriage (whether consensual, arranged, or pressured) is an adolescent girl's most likely route to sexual activity, though this is often not true for boys. A recent summary of the literature on adolescent reproductive health in India suggests (though this finding is based on admittedly unrepresentative samples) that the vast majority of sexually active adolescent girls are married (Jejeebhoy 1995).[8]

One reason we have so little information on married girls' sexual lives is the *a priori* assumption that sexual relations within marriage are consensual. Further, it is assumed that married adolescents are more knowledgeable about reproductive matters than their unmarried peers. While studies on sexuality within marriage in India are extremely rare, Jejeebhoy notes that the limited qualitative data indicate that among newly married women, who are usually adolescents, "first sexual experience with their husbands was typically described . . . as traumatic, distasteful and painful and the use of force was frequently mentioned" (Jejeebhoy 1996: 11). Surely, those who believe that adolescent fertility is "the problem" should make the experience of married adolescents a central subject of research, particularly in South and West Asia and North Africa.

Data on trends in sexual activity prior to marriage are not reliable enough to support firm conclusions about changes over time. Nonetheless, in a review of the literature in this area, McCauley and Salter state that "sexual activity among unmarried youth is increasing in many regions"

---

[8] On the other hand, the data suggest that a nontrivial number of unmarried adolescent boys—around 20–25 percent—have had sexual relations, often with older married women.

(McCauley and Salter 1995: 6). The articles cited do not provide any evidence to back this assertion; however, the absence of such data does not necessarily mean that such an increase has not taken place. Indeed, research comparing age at first sexual intercourse and age at first marriage across age cohorts reveals an increase in the gap between sexual initiation and marriage consistent with a rise in premarital sexual activity (Blanc and Way 1998). Moreover, other societal changes would predict a transformation in adolescent sexual behavior (Furstenberg 1998). The increase in school enrollment throughout the developing world—a factor likely to be contributing to the rise in women's average age at marriage—often intensifies contact between boys and girls, even where single-sex schools are the norm, and weakens parental authority. These trends, coupled with the decline in girls' average age at menarche, mean that increasing numbers of girls are exposed to the risk of sexual activity and pregnancy prior to marriage (see Chapter 1 for references regarding these trends). Furthermore, if the notion of a global youth culture has any credence, and if the United States proves to be the trendsetter in the emergence of such a culture, then the fact that rates of premarital sexual activity and childbearing have risen dramatically in the United States over the last 25 years (CDC 1991; National Center for Health Statistics 1995), although they appear to have plateaued in the 1990s (Warren et al. 1998), is further reason to anticipate changes in adolescent sexual and reproductive behavior elsewhere.[9]

While inconsistencies between reported age at first sexual intercourse and age at first marriage or consensual union or first conception are uncommon, underreporting is thought to plague survey data on the sexual behavior of adolescent girls (Blanc and Way 1998). The difficulties that adults face when interviewing other adults on sexual issues are likely to be compounded when adults try to glean first-hand information from adolescents about their sexual lives. Interviewers and respondents may feel awkward discussing premarital sexual activity, which generally is considered inappropriate behavior for females.[10] Moreover, in many developing countries, adolescents are rarely asked by outsiders (includ-

[9] While premarital sexual activity has also increased in most European countries, teenage pregnancy and childbearing rates are much lower than in the United States, largely because, according to Furstenberg (1998), the moral and political culture in Europe is less conservative and more "pragmatic." Given that there is widespread resistance in developing countries to providing reproductive health information and services to adolescents, as there has been in the United States, we might expect that rates of unprotected sex and premarital pregnancy and childbearing will rise along with premarital sexual activity rates, in keeping with the U.S., rather than the European, pattern.

[10] It is generally thought that boys, in contrast to girls, over-report sexual activity because intercourse is often seen as a badge of honor among men and a necessary rite of passage on the road to adulthood (Erulkar and Mensch 1997a).

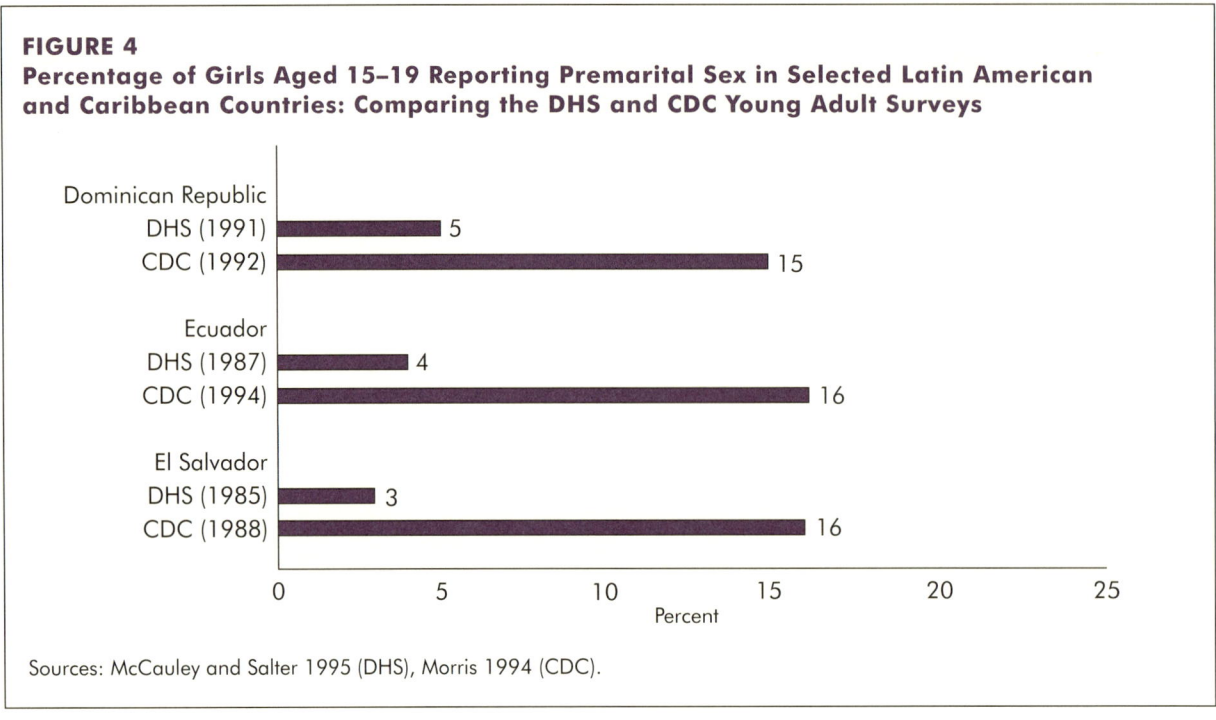

FIGURE 4
Percentage of Girls Aged 15–19 Reporting Premarital Sex in Selected Latin American and Caribbean Countries: Comparing the DHS and CDC Young Adult Surveys

Dominican Republic
DHS (1991) 5
CDC (1992) 15

Ecuador
DHS (1987) 4
CDC (1994) 16

El Salvador
DHS (1985) 3
CDC (1988) 16

0 5 10 15 20 25
Percent

Sources: McCauley and Salter 1995 (DHS), Morris 1994 (CDC).

ing teachers) to comment on any issue, least of all sexual behavior and male/female relationships. In many educational systems, passivity is encouraged among the young (Mensch and Lloyd 1998). Therefore, eliciting information from adolescents is particularly difficult; much effort must be devoted to drawing them out.[11]

Accurate reporting of adolescent sexual activity is further undermined by variable local concepts of sexual behavior and the different meanings respondents attach to such terms as partner, sex, and abstinence. Those who have had a recent sexual initiation may interpret these terms differently than those who have infrequent sexual activity (Huygens et al. 1996). Some adolescent girls may even define a sexual union according to regularity of sexual activity, the experience of a pregnancy, or even the arrival of a child.

Figure 4 compares the reporting of premarital sex among girls aged 15–19 in two surveys conducted in the same three countries. Levels of premarital sex derived from the DHS are much lower than those derived from the CDC's Young Adult Surveys—for example, 5 percent versus 15 percent in the Dominican Republic in the 1991 DHS and 1992 CDC survey, respectively. While the CDC surveys were conducted later in all three countries, this timing does not account for the large differential in report-

---

[11] Much of this section on adolescents' reporting of sexual activity draws on conversations we have had with Annabel Erulkar, based in the Population Council's office in Nairobi.

ing. In the DHS, multiple respondents in each household, including sisters and mother–daughter pairs, are interviewed about sexual activity. This explicit questioning of several family members could discourage a young, unmarried girl from reporting that she is sexually active, for fear that she will be asked later by a relative how she answered the question (Morris 1996). Surveys limited to adolescents, such as the CDC surveys, avoid this problem; moreover, interviewers trained to be attuned to adolescent concerns are probably better able to elicit valid answers to sensitive questions.

In two regions—Latin America and the Caribbean, and sub-Saharan Africa—we observe some notable variations in reported levels of sexual activity among countries that are thought to share a common culture of sexual behavior and where nonmarital sexual activity is thought to be commonplace. Figure 5 shows the percentage of women aged 20–24 reporting that they had engaged in premarital sex before age 20; it is derived from comparisons of responses to questions on age at first intercourse and age at first marriage or consensual union in 30 DHS countries. In sub-Saharan Africa, the percentage of women who report having had premarital sex as teenagers in the eight Anglophone countries— Ghana, Kenya, Namibia, Nigeria, Tanzania, Uganda, Zambia, and Zimbabwe—ranges from 26 percent to 60 percent. Nearly the same range exists in the eight Latin American and Caribbean countries (10–40 percent). The degree of variation is surprising. Unfortunately, we have no way to assess the accuracy of these data; nor do we have the contextual data necessary to understand the circumstances under which sexual intercourse is taking place and to learn who, and how old, the partners of these girls are.

The age of girls' sexual partners is significant because age differentials are thought to correspond to power differentials in sexual relationships, and a girl with less power than her partner is less able to set the terms of sexual activity and reproduction. Data on spousal age differences, which show that adolescent girls' husbands are often considerably older (see "Marriage"), suggest that unmarried girls' sexual partners are also likely to be older. One survey that gathered data on the age of girls' sexual (rather than marital) partners, conducted in Brazil, indicates that the partners of girls having first intercourse at a young age are often adult males. Among girls who had intercourse before age 15, 55 percent of their partners were six or more years older. The corresponding percentage for boys was 21 percent. While about one-quarter of boys who were sexually active before age 15 had partners the same age or younger, not one girl who was sexually active prior to that age reported a partner

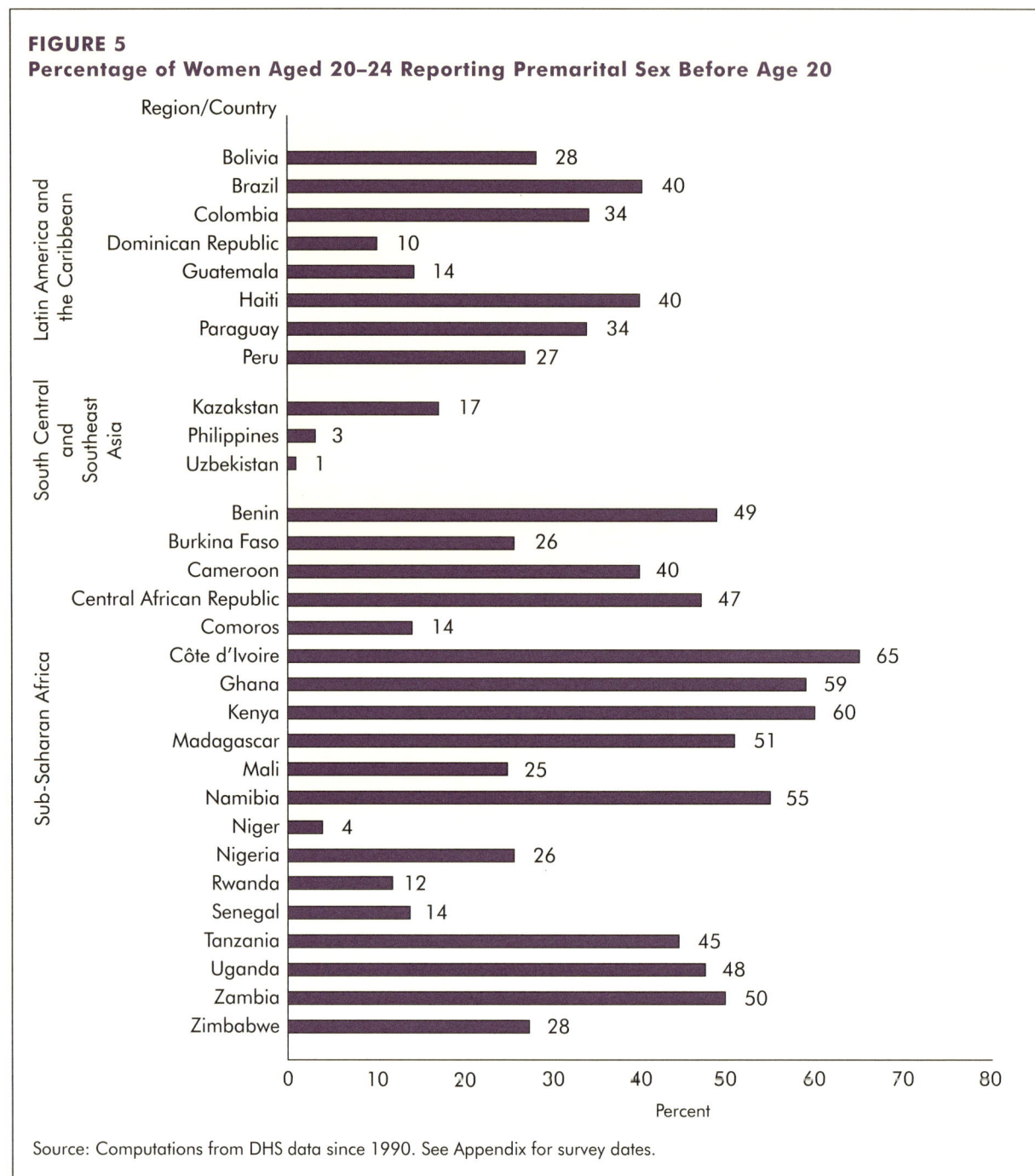

FIGURE 5
Percentage of Women Aged 20–24 Reporting Premarital Sex Before Age 20

Region/Country

Latin America and the Caribbean
- Bolivia 28
- Brazil 40
- Colombia 34
- Dominican Republic 10
- Guatemala 14
- Haiti 40
- Paraguay 34
- Peru 27

South Central and Southeast Asia
- Kazakstan 17
- Philippines 3
- Uzbekistan 1

Sub-Saharan Africa
- Benin 49
- Burkina Faso 26
- Cameroon 40
- Central African Republic 47
- Comoros 14
- Côte d'Ivoire 65
- Ghana 59
- Kenya 60
- Madagascar 51
- Mali 25
- Namibia 55
- Niger 4
- Nigeria 26
- Rwanda 12
- Senegal 14
- Tanzania 45
- Uganda 48
- Zambia 50
- Zimbabwe 28

Percent

Source: Computations from DHS data since 1990. See Appendix for survey dates.

to be the same age or younger (Bastos, Morris, and Fernandes 1989).[12] The age gap between sexual partners has become a salient concern in those developing countries where the incidence of STDs, including HIV infection, is greater among adolescent girls than among adolescent boys (e.g., Tanzania and Uganda). Indeed, there is some anecdotal evidence that where AIDS is commonplace, older men deliberately seek out younger girls in order to reduce the likelihood of becoming infected with HIV (Senderowitz 1995).[13]

A growing body of literature is drawing attention to nonconsensual sexual activity among adolescents (Boyer and Fine 1992; Laumann 1996; Stewart et al. 1996; Youri 1994). There is concern, however, that an unwillingness to acknowledge premarital sexual activity may lead adolescent girls to describe a desired sexual encounter as having been unwanted. Conversely, sexual abuse may go unreported because of fear of reprisal and shame. As noted in Chapter 2, evidence from Africa indicates that girls may use sex to help pay school fees; although this "sugar daddy" phenomenon is widely talked about, disclosure of this kind of exchange could jeopardize a girl's continuation in school.

Researchers have queried adolescents about nonconsensual sex in various ways. Some have asked very general questions—for example, "Have you ever been forced by a man to do something sexual that you did not want to do?" (Laumann 1996)—while others have posed more specific questions—for example, "Did someone ever make you touch their breasts or genitals, or touch yours, when you did not want to?" (Boyer and Fine 1992). When responses to these types of questions are tallied, the extent of coerced or forced sex that is reported is not trivial. For example, in a national sample of nearly 10,000 secondary-school girls in Kenya, one-third reported having had sexual intercourse, and approximately 40 percent of these girls indicated that their first encounter was forced or that they were "cheated into having sex" (figures are based on our tabulations of African Medical and Research Foundation data; see Youri 1994 for a description of the survey from which these data are drawn). Methodological refinements and more-extensive study may validate the reported high levels of involuntary sex among adolescent girls.

At the 1994 International Conference on Population and Development in Cairo and the 1995 Fourth World Conference on Women in Beijing, discourse on sexual and reproductive rights appropriately characterized sexual coercion as a symptom of the limited life options of girls and women. This suggests that intervention models designed to reduce sexual activity among girls must not only offer information, they must also promote public acknowledgment of the

[12] Concern about the often large age gap between adolescent girls and their sexual partners has been raised in the United States as well. A recent study of nearly 50,000 births to adolescent mothers aged 10–18 in California revealed that two-thirds of these babies were fathered by men 4–6 years older than the mothers (Males and Chew 1996).

[13] A New York Times article on the rising incidence of child rape in South Africa reported: "In recent years, the fear of AIDS has also made young girls attractive to predatory men; for a time, there was even a rumor that sex with a virgin would cure the disease" (Daley 1998: 32).

prevalence of sexual coercion and of the gender inequality that fosters it. The plausible existence of a considerable amount of nonconsensual or socially coerced adolescent sexual activity highlights the inadequacy of current intervention models, in which family planning information campaigns and services assume that sexual activity is voluntary. Much of the literature about, and information directed to, sexually active adolescents suggests they can be aided in "making better decisions." Yet, research on the effects of sexual coercion suggests that victims often have an impaired sense of autonomy, most acutely when the abuse occurred early in their lives (see, for example, Boyer and Fine 1992). As such, messages stressing responsible sexual decisionmaking may not be helpful to many adolescent girls (for more on this subject, see Chapter 4).

The deficiencies in data on adolescent sexual activity—wanted and unwanted, inside and outside of marriage—reflect and reinforce cultural denial of the facts of adolescent girls' sexual lives. Without this information, efforts to protect girls from sexually transmitted infections and from unwanted sex, pregnancy, and childbearing will be compromised. Investigators must find creative and sensitive ways to work around cultural obstacles to data collection in this area of research.[14]

Knowledge of reproductive biology and health

Wherever adolescents' knowledge of reproductive biology and health has been studied, data indicate that adolescents have a minimal grasp of this biology and a limited understanding of how to prevent pregnancy and reproductive health problems (McCauley and Salter 1995). Table 5 provides data from the DHS on adolescent girls' knowledge of ovulation—or, more specifically, when during the month a female is at greatest risk of pregnancy—in 27 of the 28 countries with never-married and ever-married respondents where this question was asked.[15] What is striking is that general levels of knowledge are not particularly high;

---

[14] In the most recent wave of the U.S. National Survey of Family Growth (NSFG), audio computer-assisted self-interviewing (known as audio CASI) was used to collect information on abortion from reproductive-age females. With this technology, the respondent listens to questions on a tape using headphones (or alternatively, reads them on a computer screen) and responds by entering her answers into the computer. According to the statistician at the National Center for Health Statistics who directs the NSFG, "pre-test respondents rated audio CASI very highly and reported more abortions using audio CASI than they reported to the interviewer" (Mosher 1998: 43). With levels of education increasing in developing regions, it may become more feasible to use this technology in research. Whether it will be as effective in increasing the level of reporting of sensitive reproductive behavior in these settings is unknown.

[15] Benin is the one country with never-married and ever-married respondents that is excluded from Table 5 because there were fewer than 20 respondents with 4–7 years of schooling.

TABLE 5

Percentage of Girls Aged 15–19 With 4-7 Years of Schooling Who Correctly Identified the Time of Month When Ovulation Is Most Likely to Occur

Region/Country	Ever married	Never married
Latin America and the Caribbean		
Brazil	29	34
Colombia	32	46
Dominican Republic	10	11
Guatemala	8	10
Haiti	4	9
Paraguay	19	21
Peru	35	29
South Central and Southeast Asia		
Kazakstan	25	7
Philippines	29	13
Uzbekistan	6	1
Sub-Saharan Africa		
Burkina Faso	23	16
Cameroon	28	31
Central African Republic	21	11
Comoros	28	12
Côte d'Ivoire	43	44
Ghana	15	14
Kenya	16	12
Madagascar	30	24
Malawi	12	11
Mali	6	13
Namibia	6	2
Niger	11	8
Nigeria	9	19
Rwanda	10	10
Senegal	6	10
Tanzania	16	4
Zambia	10	6

Source: Computations from DHS data since 1990. See Appendix for survey dates.

nowhere could at least half of 15–19-year-olds identify the time of month when ovulation is most likely to occur and pregnancy risk is highest. In analyzing the DHS data, we separated respondents by marital status and controlled for years of schooling—limiting the analysis to those with 4–7 years of education—because we wanted to determine whether ever-married females were more knowledgeable about ovulation than never-married females, and because those who marry early are usually less educated than their unmarried peers. We found that married females, who presumably are having sex more regularly, generally are not more knowledgeable about this subject.

Familiarity with other aspects of reproductive biology is also likely to be poor. A survey of unmarried adolescents visiting youth centers in Nairobi and Mombasa, Kenya found that awareness of the pregnancy risk associated with the practice of withdrawal was as low as knowledge of the timing of ovulation (Erulkar and Mensch 1997b). (For a discussion of adolescents' knowledge of modern contraceptive methods, see "Fertility regulation.")

Adolescents' knowledge of reproductive health problems, and how to protect against them, is likewise limited. For example, the survey of Kenyan adolescents revealed that respondents were susceptible to rumors concerning the protective effect of condoms, despite generally being aware of how HIV is transmitted. Approximately one-third thought that condoms have small holes to allow HIV to pass through, and a similar percentage thought that condoms are laced with HIV (Erulkar and Mensch 1997b).

Adolescent girls' knowledge of reproductive biology and health is critical to their ability to protect themselves from unwanted reproductive outcomes. While such knowledge is not sufficient to prevent such outcomes (as noted in our discussion of sexual coercion), it is every girl's right and need to possess this information. Girls and boys should know, at the very least, how pregnancy happens, how STDs are spread, and what measures can be taken to prevent unwanted pregnancy and sexually transmitted infection.

Fertility regulation

Despite their limited knowledge of reproductive biology and health, young people generally know about at least one modern contraceptive method, and a surprising proportion—over half in 16 of 25 countries—know where they can obtain such a method, according to our analysis of DHS data (see Table 6).[16] However, as is extensively documented, knowledge of a method may be insufficient for its safe and effective use (McCauley and Salter 1995; McDevitt et al. 1996; Senderowitz 1995; WHO and UNICEF 1995). Furthermore, knowledge of a supply source hardly guarantees that the method will be obtained.

Analyses of adolescent contraceptive use have usually focused on use prior to marriage, as premarital sexual encounters are viewed as inherently risky. Figure 6 shows the percentage of never-married girls aged 15–19 who are currently sexually active and are practicing contra-

---

[16] Because knowledge of contraception is very high among both never-married and ever-married respondents, we did not feel it necessary to control for years of schooling in order to compare the two groups.

ception in the 17 DHS countries where sufficient, albeit small, numbers of girls in this age group report sexual activity in the four weeks prior to the survey. Given the low levels of modern contraceptive use in all countries other than Brazil and Kazakstan, the vast majority of these girls are at some risk of pregnancy. How great this risk is depends on levels of sub-fecundity, particularly among younger adolescents, and frequency of sex, which is typically low in this age group.[17]

Self-reports of fertility regulation by adolescents may not be representative of contraceptive use in this age group, given that girls willing to acknowledge having had intercourse may constitute a selective sample. The nature and magnitude of the bias of their reporting are unknown; however, it seems likely that girls who are comfortable enough to report sexual activity would be more inclined to use a contraceptive method (because one of the barriers to adolescent girls' contraceptive use is embarrassment and even guilt about their sexual activity). If so, contraceptive use among sexually active adolescents may be overestimated by the DHS and other survey data.

The low level of contraceptive use among adolescents in developing countries is not satisfactorily explained by DHS data. Researchers have assumed that nonuse among those who are unmarried, sexually active, and not pregnant signals an unmet need for family planning (Westoff and Bankole 1995). Among adolescents, this presumed unmet need is generally attributed to inadequate knowledge of contraception; sporadic or unanticipated sexual activity; deficient services; and judgmental and insensitive family planning workers (McCauley and Salter 1995). All of the above conditions are well known and undoubtedly do obstruct adolescent contraceptive use. However, for some adolescent girls, pregnancy may be accepted, or at least not dreaded, because it demonstrates fecundity and could encourage a male partner to make a more permanent commitment (Bledsoe and Cohen 1993; Calvès, Cornwell, and Enyegue 1996). For other girls, contraception is not an option because they have limited power to negotiate its use, or because their sexual activity is coerced (McCauley and Salter 1995). Thus, while many sexually active unmarried girls who are not practicing contraception may, indeed, have an "unmet need for family planning" as conventionally defined, they have much broader needs that are not being met, some of which bear on their fertility behavior. (See "Marriage" for a discussion of unmet need for family planning among married adolescents.)

> While many sexually active unmarried girls may have an "unmet need for family planning," they have much broader needs that are not being met, some of which bear on their fertility behavior.

---

[17] For data documenting the sporadic nature of adolescent sex in the United States, see Moore et al. (1987).

TABLE 6

Percentage of Ever-Married and Never-Married Girls Aged 15–19 With Knowledge of a Modern Contraceptive Method and Its Source

Region/Country	Ever/never married	Knows of method	Knows of source
Latin America and the Caribbean			
Bolivia	ever	68	40
	never	69	31
Brazil	ever	100	*
	never	99	*
Colombia	ever	99	89
	never	99	79
Dominican Republic	ever	100	93
	never	99	91
Guatemala	ever	67	**
	never	68	**
Haiti	ever	100	*
	never	94	*
Paraguay	ever	84	71
	never	94	84
Peru	ever	86	72
	never	90	80
South Central and Southeast Asia			
Bangladesh	ever	99	93
Indonesia	ever	96	**
Kazakstan	ever	91	**
	never	97	**
Nepal	ever	97	**
Pakistan	ever	66	32
Philippines	ever	89	84
	never	92	77
Uzbekistan	ever	65	**
	never	86	**
Sub-Saharan Africa			
Benin	ever	69	**
	never	67	**
Burkina Faso	ever	61	26
	never	53	22
Cameroon	ever	60	42
	never	73	53
Central African Republic	ever	70	**
	never	55	**
Comoros	ever	97	**
	never	91	**
Côte d'Ivoire	ever	72	**
	never	83	**
Ghana	ever	86	62
	never	84	57
Kenya	ever	97	88
	never	89	69

continued

TABLE 6
(continued)

Region/Country	Ever/never married	Knows of method	Knows of source
Sub-Saharan Africa (continued)			
Madagascar	ever	43	28
	never	38	24
Malawi	ever	65	49
	never	86	74
Mali	ever	65	**
	never	65	**
Namibia	ever	77	60
	never	90	85
Niger	ever	50	26
	never	49	22
Nigeria	ever	32	24
	never	43	32
Rwanda	ever	94	70
	never	99	85
Senegal	ever	60	26
	never	59	32
Tanzania	ever	60	**
	never	81	**
Uganda	ever	92	63
	never	78	71
Zambia	ever	85	**
	never	94	**
Zimbabwe	ever	97	80
	never	93	58
West Asia and North Africa			
Egypt	ever	98	83
Morocco	ever	99	90
	never	93	**
Turkey	ever	98	90
Yemen	ever	51	24

* Question asks about source for any method.
** Question not asked.

Note: Married girls include those formally married and those living with their male partner.

Source: Computations from DHS data since 1990. See Appendix for survey dates.

The number of adolescent girls seeking abortions is a powerful, if indirect, indicator of unwanted pregnancy. Estimating rates of abortions and ratios of abortions to pregnancies is enormously problematic, however, even in countries where abortion is legal, because of societal and religious sanctions against abortion, which compromise the collection of accurate data (Singh and Henshaw 1996). Demographers have devised a number of procedures to estimate aggregate levels of abortion on a country-wide basis (see, for example, Johnston and Hill

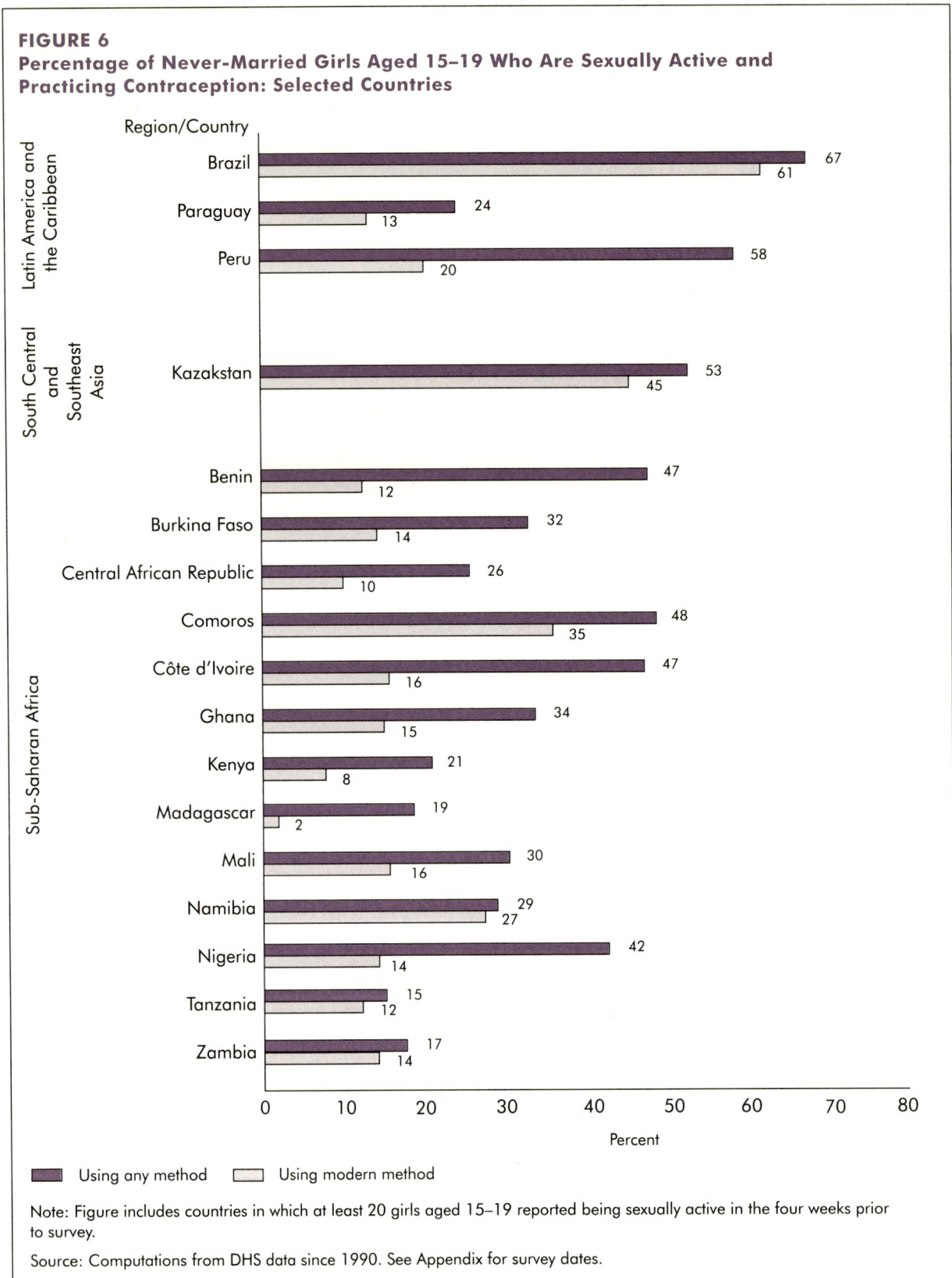

FIGURE 6
Percentage of Never-Married Girls Aged 15–19 Who Are Sexually Active and Practicing Contraception: Selected Countries

Region/Country

Latin America and the Caribbean

Brazil — 67 / 61
Paraguay — 24 / 13
Peru — 58 / 20

South Central and Southeast Asia

Kazakstan — 53 / 45

Sub-Saharan Africa

Benin — 47 / 12
Burkina Faso — 32 / 14
Central African Republic — 26 / 10
Comoros — 48 / 35
Côte d'Ivoire — 47 / 16
Ghana — 34 / 15
Kenya — 21 / 8
Madagascar — 19 / 2
Mali — 30 / 16
Namibia — 29 / 27
Nigeria — 42 / 14
Tanzania — 15 / 12
Zambia — 17 / 14

Percent

■ Using any method   □ Using modern method

Note: Figure includes countries in which at least 20 girls aged 15–19 reported being sexually active in the four weeks prior to survey.

Source: Computations from DHS data since 1990. See Appendix for survey dates.

1996; Singh and Wulf 1994). Rarely, however, are estimates generated for separate age groups.

Although abortion is common among adolescents in many countries, two of the leading experts on the measurement of abortion argue that the vast majority of abortion clients in many developing countries are married, adult women with children, who want to delay the next birth or terminate childbearing altogether. Conversely, in developed countries, a disproportionate share of abortion clients are adolescents. Singh and Henshaw cite data from the United States and England, where about one-quarter of abortion clients are under age 20, and data from four Latin American countries (Bolivia, Colombia, Peru, and Venezuela) and India, where respectively 12 percent and 5 percent of abortion clients are that young. In many countries in the Middle East and South Asia (they use India as an example), unmarried girls are rarely sexually active and, thus, are not at risk of having an abortion. In Latin America, where premarital sex is more common, adolescent pregnancy often results in a consensual union or marriage and is, thus, less likely to terminate in abortion (Singh and Henshaw 1996).

While abortion rates may be lower for adolescent girls than for older women, Singh and Wulf note that in the four Latin American countries where data are available, adolescents are over-represented among females hospitalized for abortion complications (using the proportion of adolescents hospitalized for childbirth as a comparative base). The younger the abortion patient, the greater the likelihood of sepsis (probably due to a delay in seeking medical care): one-third of patients under age 20 presented with sepsis, compared to 15 percent of those aged 35–39 (Singh and Wulf 1993). Hirsch and Barker compiled abortion data from 27 studies in developing countries (drawn largely from urban, hospital-based samples) and found that adolescent admissions accounted for 60 percent of females admitted with abortion-related complications. They claim that adolescent girls comprise a substantial share of the estimated 100,000–200,000 deaths attributable to abortion complications in developing countries each year (Hirsch and Barker 1992). Singh and Henshaw's estimate of abortion-related deaths in developing countries is lower by half: 50,000–100,000 per year. Moreover, they maintain that adolescents comprise considerably less than 60 percent of hospital patients admitted for abortion-related complications. They estimate the proportion of adolescent abortion patients to be around 10–20 percent in six Latin American countries representing 70 percent of the region's population (Singh and Henshaw 1996).

> **The transition to marriage often consumes many years of a girl's adolescence, compromising her schooling and livelihood choices.**

Singh notes that data on adolescent abortion are so uncertain that she is unwilling to estimate the total number of abortions to adolescents worldwide (Singh 1998a). These uncertainties, which are reflected in the discrepancies between researchers' findings in this area, point to the difficulty of collecting data on the sensitive subject of adolescent abortion—indeed, on adolescent fertility regulation in general.

Marriage

Marriage is a vital category of interest because of its impact on the quality of adolescent girls' lives. In many societies, the transition to marriage—for example, the period in which an unmarried girl prepares to become a wife—often consumes many years of a girl's adolescence, compromising her schooling and livelihood choices. This situation reflects girls' limited power in many developing countries to make their own marital and reproductive choices.

Demographers have been particularly interested in women's age at marriage because, for most females in the developing world, it is closely linked to their age at childbirth. Moreover, early marriage is associated with limited education and work experience, a premature end to girls' "personal growth," and higher rates of separation and divorce (Singh and Samara 1996: 148). The links between these factors and age at marriage are often assumed to be causal; however, this is difficult to determine in the absence of longitudinal data.

Demographers tend to treat marriage as a firm boundary: an event that occurs at a fixed point in time and carries a universal meaning. This is not an appropriate characterization of marriage in all cultures, however. In parts of sub-Saharan Africa (Botswana, for example), formal marriage may not take place until a couple's children are themselves nearing young adulthood (Bledsoe and Cohen 1993). Even where marriage is viewed as a necessary antecedent to pregnancy and childbirth, the marriage process may be protracted. For example, among some ethnic groups in Côte d'Ivoire, the marriage ceremony precedes cohabitation and sexual relations by at least several months. Girls' mean age at the time of this ceremony is 13–14 years; nearly one-fifth of marrying girls are younger than 11 (Meekers 1992).

The relative timing of sexual activity, cohabitation, and marriage is a subject of increasing research. Studies in developed countries of changing norms of sexuality have often included young people's attitudes toward cohabitation and its place in the marital process. Researchers typically find that partner consensus concerning the prospect of marriage is very high among cohabiting couples.[18] Studies along these lines are beginning to be conducted in developing countries, where rates of unmarried sexual activity may be rising, suggesting a concomitant increase in premarital cohabitation; but marriage undoubtedly remains a goal for most young people. Research in the Philippines, where there is substantial premarital sex, shows that most sexual activity outside marriage takes place within committed relationships leading to marriage, rather than in casual relationships. Single Filipino females are reluctant to admit having had premarital sex—only 2 percent did so in a 1994 national survey that sampled 10,000 young adults; yet, among females classified as formally married at the time of the survey, about half reported having lived with their spouse prior to marriage (Xenos 1997).

Latin America and the Caribbean may present a different picture with respect to cohabitation and marriage. Rather than being a stage prior to marriage, cohabitation may often be a substitute for marriage—albeit an unstable one—in this region. Surveys conducted in the 1970s showed that women in Colombia, Panama, and Peru who had been in consensual unions were much more likely than women who were legally married to report that their relationship had dissolved within 20 years. While these data are quite old, the researchers who cite them report that "there is little reason to think that this situation . . . has changed much since the mid-1970s" (Singh and Wulf 1990). Moreover, they argue that there has been an increase in consensual unions among teenagers—a worrisome development given the high rates of dissolution among these unions.

In many African and South Asian settings, families are closely involved in the selection of marital partners and in the implicit or explicit contract that marriage signifies. In rural sub-Saharan Africa, protracted negotiation between families over bridewealth (also known as brideprice) is an integral feature of the marriage process (Kuper 1982). In South Asia, arranged marriage remains the norm.

Over the last 30 years, dowry has increasingly replaced bridewealth in South Asia.[19] This is believed to be a consequence of a "marriage squeeze"—a deficiency of marriageable (that is, older) men for younger and larger[20] cohorts of females. This trend has negative consequences

---

[18] In the United States, 80 percent of currently cohabiting young adults interviewed in a national survey expect to marry their current partners (Sweet and Bumpass 1990). Within four years of initiating cohabitation, two-thirds of Caucasians in the United States marry their partners (Manning and Smock 1995).

[19] Bridewealth/brideprice is paid in cash or kind by the groom's family to the bride's family. Dowry is brought by the bride to the groom's family.

[20] as a result of population growth.

for girls, as it renders them more of an economic burden on their families than in the past (Amin and Cain 1997; Caldwell, Reddy, and Caldwell 1983).

A study of female autonomy and relations within marriage in Egypt found evidence of an inverse relationship between familial involvement in spouse selection and female age at marriage. Among females who married before the legal age of 16—who comprised about 40 percent of currently married females—only one in 10 chose their husband; by comparison, 40 percent of those who married after age 25 chose their husband (Nawar, Lloyd, and Ibrahim 1995).

In this study sample, a large majority (75 percent) of Egyptian mothers expected their daughters to marry by age 20; however, they also believed that their daughters should have no more than two children. This phenomenon is of special interest because it suggests that parents' attachment to the ideal of early marriage for daughters may not be closely connected to fertility goals. If the decision to marry, or parents' pressure for marriage, had been formed around the expectation of high fertility, then marriage could be pushed far past age 20 with little risk of females failing to achieve desired fertility levels. Yet, in Egypt, where desired family size has fallen below three children, females' median age at marriage is 19 (El-Zanaty et al. 1996). This suggests that the cultural ideal of early marriage and early childbearing is linked to gender-role expectations for girls, rather than to fertility goals.

Macro-level data support this hypothesis to some extent. Table 7 indicates that in the 19 countries where there has been at least a half-year rise in women's average age at marriage, there has not been a parallel increase in the time elapsed between marriage and first birth; such an increase might be expected if delayed marriage marked a broader trend away from traditional gender roles. Where women's average age at first birth has risen, it is entirely attributable to an increase in women's average age at marriage, not to a postponement of childbearing within marriage. The interval between marriage and first birth has either diminished or remained constant (at 1–2 years) in countries where women's age at marriage has increased. Moreover, in 16 of the 20 countries where women's age at marriage has remained the same or even fallen, the interval between marriage and first birth has remained constant or declined. Only in countries where females' age at marriage is very low—a median of around age 17 or below—is the average interval between marriage and first birth greater than two years, presumably the result of adolescent subfecundity. In short, marriage and first birth are still closely linked in most settings.

The urgency to marry and have children early is related to the precariousness of girls' status. In many societies, if a female fails to give birth within a few years of marriage, she encounters difficulties with her husband and in-laws and may receive less care and support from them; she may even be rejected or physically harmed if customary norms of childbearing are not observed. Kakar reports that in India, "[w]hether her family is poor or wealthy, whatever her caste, class or region, whether she is a fresh young bride or exhausted by many pregnancies and infancies already, an Indian woman knows that motherhood confers upon her a purpose and identity that nothing else in her culture can . . ." (1981: 57). Despite rising levels of female education and more flexible sexual behaviors, females' traditional mandate to begin bearing children soon after marriage remains integral to their respectability and economic security in many societies.

Because motherhood remains fundamental to female identity, the data on unmet need for family planning among married adolescents are difficult to interpret. According to our analysis of DHS data, 15 percent of married 15–19-year-old girls without any children in Egypt, and 29 percent in Pakistan, have this unmet need. But when a married adolescent in Egypt or Pakistan, who faces clear familial and societal expectations to reproduce, tells an interviewer that she does not want to be pregnant now but is not practicing contraception, the problem may not be that the family planning program is failing to meet her needs; rather, it may be that she lacks the power within her marriage to act on her desire to use the contraceptive services that are available to her. Thus, these data on unmet need are of questionable validity, given the pervasive pressure on young, childless wives to bear children. While the concept of unmet need is undergoing scrutiny in the family planning field—several in-depth studies on this topic are being fielded (Casterline, Perez, and Biddlecom 1997; ICRW 1997)—it probably has the least utility in its application to young, married females, and requires the most investigation in this area, on the demand and supply sides. As for the latter, there is cross-regional evidence that when young, married females seek fertility regulation services in conservative, high-fertility societies, they encounter substantial, often explicit, provider resistance (Huntington, Lettenmaier, and Obeng-Quaidoo 1990; Ibrahim 1995; Rajaretnam and Deshpande 1994).

TABLE 7
Women's Median Age at Marriage and Median Number of Months Between Marriage and First Birth by Age Group

Region/Country		Age group			
		25–29	30–34	35–39	40–44
Latin America and the Caribbean					
Bolivia	age at marriage	20.0	20.1	20.6	20.7
	months between marriage and first birth	14	15	16	17
Brazil	age at marriage	21.0	21.0	21.0	21.0
	months between marriage and first birth	21	20	19	17
Colombia	age at marriage	21.6	21.6	21.3	21.4
	months between marriage and first birth	16	17	15	13
Dominican Republic	age at marriage	19.8	19.4	18.8	18.4
	months between marriage and first birth	17	17	18	17
Guatemala	age at marriage	19.1	18.5	18.6	19.2
	months between marriage and first birth	14	15	15	15
Haiti	age at marriage	20.5	20.7	20.6	21.4
	months between marriage and first birth	15	15	15	14
Paraguay	age at marriage	20.8	20.8	21.7	20.6
	months between marriage and first birth	16	17	17	18
Peru	age at marriage	21.8	21.2	21.0	20.6
	months between marriage and first birth	13	14	14	13
South Central and Southeast Asia					
Bangladesh*	age at marriage	14.7	14.2	13.9	13.6
	months between marriage and first birth	29	34	36	35
Indonesia*	age at marriage	19.1	18.2	17.9	17.3
	months between marriage and first birth	17	17	20	22
Kazakstan	age at marriage	21.2	21.3	21.0	20.9
	months between marriage and first birth	11	12	11	12
Nepal	age at marriage	16.5	16.4	16.2	15.8
	months between marriage and first birth	28	31	38	39
Pakistan*	age at marriage	18.8	18.2	18.6	18.5
	months between marriage and first birth	20	21	21	24
Philippines	age at marriage	22.0	21.7	21.4	21.5
	months between marriage and first birth	13	13	12	14
Uzbekistan	age at marriage[3]	20.0	20.4	19.9	19.7
	months between marriage and first birth	14	14	14	14
Sub-Saharan Africa					
Benin	age at marriage	18.7	18.3	18.5	18.3
	months between marriage and first birth	17	16	17	17
Burkina Faso	age at marriage	17.5	17.5	17.5	17.5
	months between marriage and first birth	23	22	22	22
Cameroon	age at marriage	16.9	16.6	16.6	16.3
	months between marriage and first birth	26	24	34	35
Central African Republic	age at marriage	17.4	17.3	17.8	16.6
	months between marriage and first birth	20	20	21	20
Comoros	age at marriage	20.4	18.4	18.2	17.6
	months between marriage and first birth	21	22	25	24
Côte d'Ivoire	age at marriage	18.2	18.1	18.0	18.2
	months between marriage and first birth	22	20	21	23

continued

TABLE 7
(continued)

Region/Country		Age group			
		25–29	30–34	35–39	40–44
Sub-Saharan Africa (continued)					
Ghana	age at marriage	18.9	18.6	19.0	18.7
	months between marriage and first birth	17	19	19	16
Kenya	age at marriage	19.5	18.9	18.2	18.3
	months between marriage and first birth	14	18	16	20
Madagascar	age at marriage	18.9	18.2	18.0	18.0
	months between marriage and first birth	17	16	17	17
Malawi	age at marriage	17.7	17.2	17.9	18.1
	months between marriage and first birth	16	16	17	17
Mali	age at marriage	16.1	16.0	16.1	15.9
	months between marriage and first birth	24	24	27	31
Namibia	age at marriage	26.8	24.9	24.0	24.4
	months between marriage and first birth	18	17	16	17
Niger	age at marriage	14.9	14.9	15.1	14.8
	months between marriage and first birth	35	35	39	44
Nigeria	age at marriage	17.2	16.3	17.3	16.9
	months between marriage and first birth	26	24	27	27
Rwanda	age at marriage	20.9	20.2	20.0	19.4
	months between marriage and first birth	15	15	17	16
Senegal	age at marriage	16.8	16.2	16.1	15.8
	months between marriage and first birth	26	24	33	36
Tanzania	age at marriage	18.8	18.6	17.6	17.4
	months between marriage and first birth	15	16	16	15
Uganda	age at marriage	18.9	18.6	19.0	18.7
	months between marriage and first birth	18	17	16	18
Zambia	age at marriage	18.4	17.9	17.4	17.4
	months between marriage and first birth	15	16	14	16
Zimbabwe	age at marriage	19.3	18.7	18.8	18.9
	months between marriage and first birth	14	14	14	16
West Asia and North Africa					
Egypt*	age at marriage	19.8	19.3	19.3	18.9
	months between marriage and first birth	15	16	16	18
Morocco	age at marriage	22.3	20.0	19.4	18.6
	months between marriage and first birth	18	20	22	22
Turkey*	age at marriage	19.2	18.8	18.5	18.4
	months between marriage and first birth	14	14	15	17
Yemen*	age at marriage	16.1	15.7	15.7	15.7
	months between marriage and first birth	34	35	49	49

* Sample is restricted to ever-married women; assume 50 percent of women were married and gave birth by age 25.

Note: Marriage is defined to include formal marriage and cohabitation with a male partner. Women who gave birth prior to marriage or less than eight months after marriage and those who are not married are excluded from the analysis of the interval between marriage and first birth. The birth restriction eliminates women for whom pregnancy or birth might have driven the decision to marry. The marriage restriction will only make a difference in the 25–29-year age group and even then it should not make a large difference in the median number of months between marriage and first birth, as the vast majority of women in these countries are married by ages 25–29.

Source: Computations from DHS data since 1990. See Appendix for survey dates.

Figure 7 shows the percentage of women aged 25–29 who had married by age 18 in the 39 DHS countries included in our analysis.[21] While the incidence of early marriage varies considerably and is declining in all regions of the developing world (Singh and Samara 1996), the proportion of females married by age 18 is still at least 25 percent in six of eight Latin American and Caribbean countries, four of seven South Central and Southeast Asian countries, 18 of 20 sub-Saharan African countries, and 3 of 4 West Asian and North African countries; in 12 countries—9 in sub-Saharan Africa—this proportion exceeds 50 percent. If the definition of childhood in the Convention on the Rights of the Child—namely, that it extends through age 18—is applied here, these data reveal stunningly high levels of child marriage, particularly in parts of Asia and North and sub-Saharan Africa.

Not only do many females marry while they are still legally children, but these girls often marry men who are considerably older. (Males are generally not encouraged to marry while they are still adolescents; thus, males, unlike females, rarely marry before reaching adulthood.) Table 8 shows the age difference between spouses in Colombia, Egypt, and Turkey for women aged 20–29 who had married as adolescents (that is, prior to age 20) and for women aged 30–39 who had married in their 20s. Although spousal age differences vary, in all three countries the husband is likely to be substantially older than his wife if she married as an adolescent. Indeed, the gap between spouses' ages is often considerably greater when the bride is under 20. In Egypt, where the average spousal age difference is the largest, 65 percent of adolescent brides marry men more than five years older than they are, and nearly one-quarter marry men 10 or more years older. Among women who marry in their 20s, the comparable figures are 43 percent and 12 percent. That the age difference between spouses is larger for females who marry as adolescents is

---

[21] In the interest of documenting current behavior, we would have preferred to show data from the youngest females whose experience is not censored—that is, those aged 18–25. However, seven of the countries included in our analysis limit their samples to married females. Younger females in these surveys are not representative of all females their age because single females are excluded from the samples. Thus, for purposes of comparability, we restricted our analysis for all countries to women aged 25–29. While virtually all females in these seven countries marry, and most do so by age 25, there are still sufficient numbers who marry after age 25 (in five of the seven countries—Bangladesh and Nepal are the exceptions) to affect estimates of the proportion of females married by age 18. We used DHS estimates of the proportion married by ages 25–29 (which are based on household listings of marital status by age) to deflate the proportions married by age 18. So, for example, 35 percent of ever-married women aged 25–29 in Egypt had married by age 18; however, 13 percent of women in that age group have not yet married, which means that approximately 30 percent of all women aged 25–29 had married by age 18.

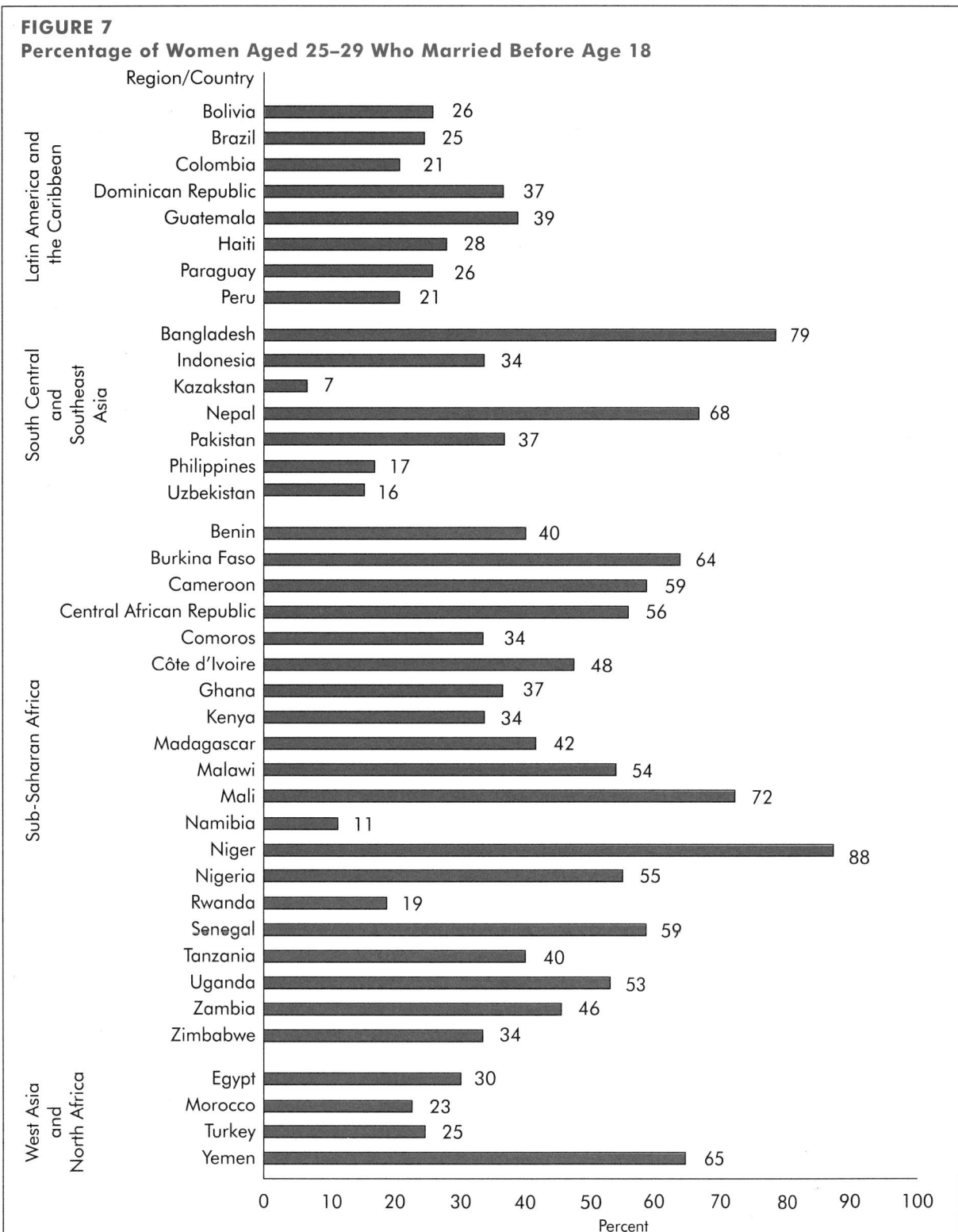

FIGURE 7
Percentage of Women Aged 25–29 Who Married Before Age 18

Note: Sample is restricted to ever-married women. Percentages are deflated by the proportions estimated to be married by ages 25–29 in order to ensure comparability with samples that include never-married women. Those proportions are: .978 in Bangladesh, .866 in Egypt, .860 in Indonesia, .954 in Nepal, .856 in Pakistan, .844 in Turkey, and .909 in Yemen. For more on the procedure used to compare samples of all women with samples restricted to ever-married women, see footnote 21 to this chapter.

Source: Computations from DHS data since 1990. See Appendix for survey dates.

TABLE 8

Spousal Age Differences for Women Aged 20–29 and 30–39 by Women's Age at Marriage: Colombia, Egypt, and Turkey

	Women aged 20–29 married before age 20 (%)			Women aged 30–39 married between ages 20–29 (%)		
	Colombia	Egypt	Turkey	Colombia	Egypt	Turkey
Husband younger than wife	5.7	0.8	3.1	21.9	7.1	16.5
Husband same age as wife	5.3	1.4	4.2	12.6	7.1	12.5
Husband 1–5 years older	45.9	33.2	47.9	38.4	42.8	54.5
Husband 6–10 years older	25.5	40.3	37.7	16.6	30.7	11.3
Husband 10+ years older	17.6	24.4	7.1	10.4	12.4	5.2

Note: Marriage is defined to include formal marriage and cohabitation with a male partner.

Source: Computations from DHS data since 1990. See Appendix for survey dates.

not simply attributable to the fact that early-marrying females are from lower socioeconomic groups, in which it is normative for girls to marry much older men. The inverse relationship between spousal age difference and wife's age at marriage is maintained even when education of the woman is controlled—indeed, education has little effect (see Figure 8). Thus, women who marry in their 20s have spouses who are closer in age than equally educated women who marry earlier.

Given the magnitude of spousal age differences for married, adolescent girls, it is reasonable to assume that many teenage brides have limited capacity to negotiate with their husbands about sex, contraception, and childbearing, as well as other aspects of domestic life. In Bangladesh, "[large] age differences between spouses, particularly when the bride is little more than a child, . . . can increase the level of awe in the bride and her deference towards the husband-god (*poti-debota*) that is idealized in Bengali culture" (Amin and Cain 1997: 301).

While spousal age differences are suggestive of imbalances between husbands and their young wives, we have few direct means to verify this, however, there is a precedent in the literature for regarding these differences as a measure of the level of equity within marriage. In his cross-cultural analysis of women's status and fertility, Cain uses spousal age differences as a parsimonious indicator of patriarchal structure. "In general, a large difference in age of spouses . . . connotes a potentially powerful means of male control over women," he argues (1984: 39–40).

Our insights into girls' experience in the early stages of marriage are limited. One recent study in Egypt revealed that, even among girls who have been involved in a community development and income-generating scheme for an average of two to three years, the first year of marriage was experienced as a "setback, and in some cases, as virtual bondage"

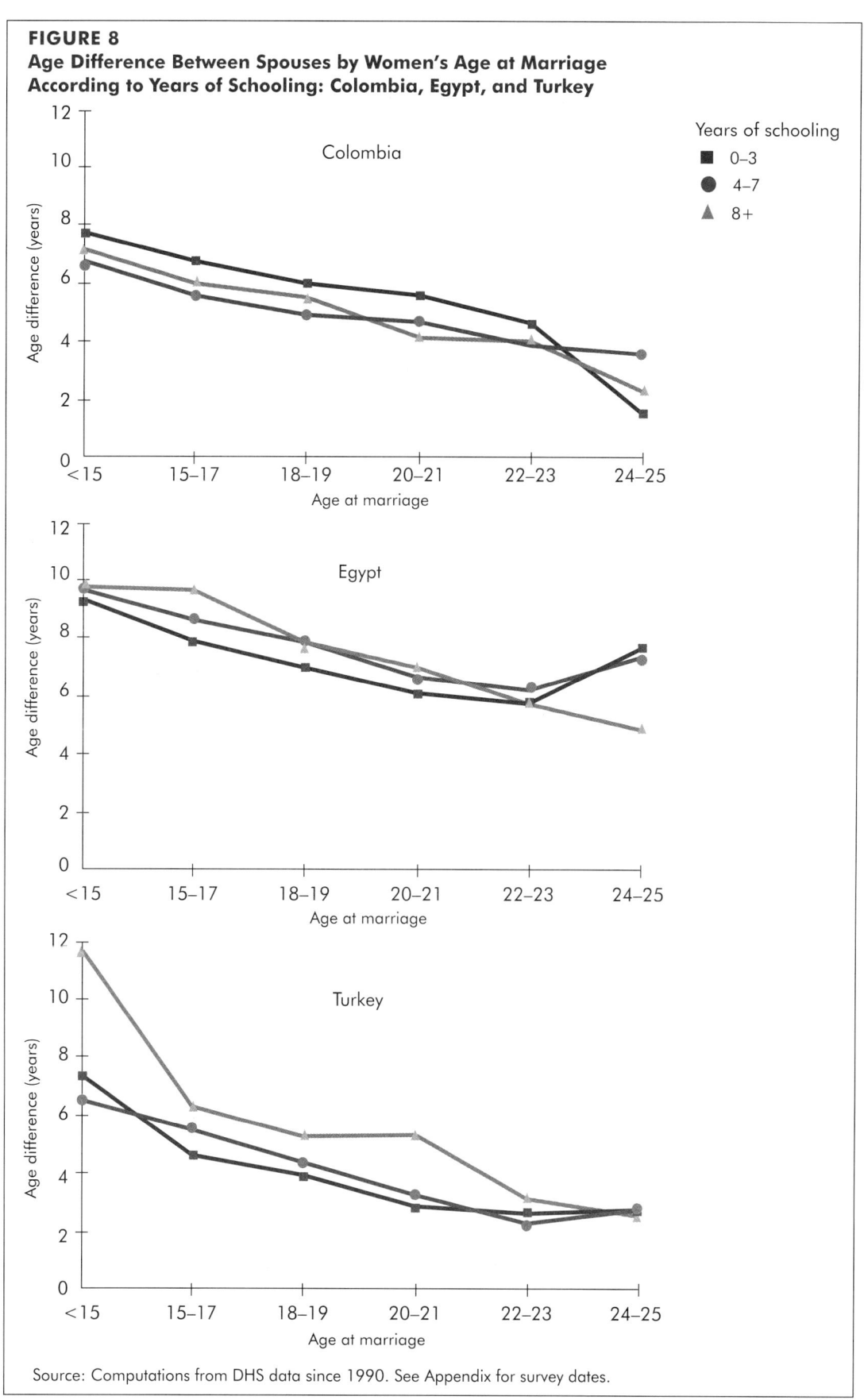

FIGURE 8

Age Difference Between Spouses by Women's Age at Marriage According to Years of Schooling: Colombia, Egypt, and Turkey

Years of schooling
■ 0–3
● 4–7
▲ 8+

Colombia

Age difference (years)

<15   15–17   18–19   20–21   22–23   24–25

Age at marriage

Egypt

Age difference (years)

<15   15–17   18–19   20–21   22–23   24–25

Age at marriage

Turkey

Age difference (years)

<15   15–17   18–19   20–21   22–23   24–25

Age at marriage

Source: Computations from DHS data since 1990. See Appendix for survey dates.

(Assaad and Bruce 1997: 20). Additional qualitative research on the lives of married adolescent girls is needed, including studies of newly married couples' sexual relations, fertility decisionmaking, social mobility, control over financial resources, workload, and time use.

The lack of research, policy, and programmatic attention to married adolescent girls reflects the pervasive—and, in our view, profoundly misleading—assumption that girls' childhood ends, and adulthood begins, with marriage and/or childbearing. We maintain that a girl remains an adolescent—with stage-specific vulnerabilities, capacities, and developmental opportunities—roughly from the time she turns 10 until she turns 20, whether or not she marries or gives birth. Recognition of this fact will help to bring much-deserved attention to the large proportion of adolescent girls who become wives before they become adults.

Childbearing

Adolescent childbearing has declined in the last few decades, yet substantial numbers of females still give birth in their teenage years. Figure 9 shows the percentage of women aged 25–29 who had given birth by age 20 in the 39 DHS countries included in our analysis.[22] In every country except Kazakstan, at least one-fifth of these women gave birth as teenagers, and in 19 countries (16 of them in sub-Saharan Africa) more than half gave birth before age 20.

In our analysis of DHS data, we divided women according to whether their child was conceived within or prior to a marriage or consensual union. Those who became pregnant before marriage are further separated into those who married before the birth and those who did not. This shows that, in sub-Saharan Africa and Latin America, children born to adolescent girls are often conceived, and frequently born, prior to marriage. In other words, for many females, pregnancy does not lead immediately to marriage. For example, in Brazil, over 40 percent of women who gave birth prior to age 20 either conceived or gave birth before they married. In Kenya, this was true of more than half of these women.

The widespread belief that premarital childbearing is rising among developing-country adolescents is not borne out by the data. Surveys in most countries in Africa and Latin America do not indicate an increase

---

[22] As with marriage, we would have preferred to show data from the youngest cohorts included in the samples whose experience is not censored (those aged 20–25). However, because of selectivity problems in five countries limited to married women (see previous footnote), we had to raise the lower age boundary to 25. We also deflated the proportions of women aged 25–29 who gave birth by age 20 by multiplying by the percentage of women aged 25–29 who are married.

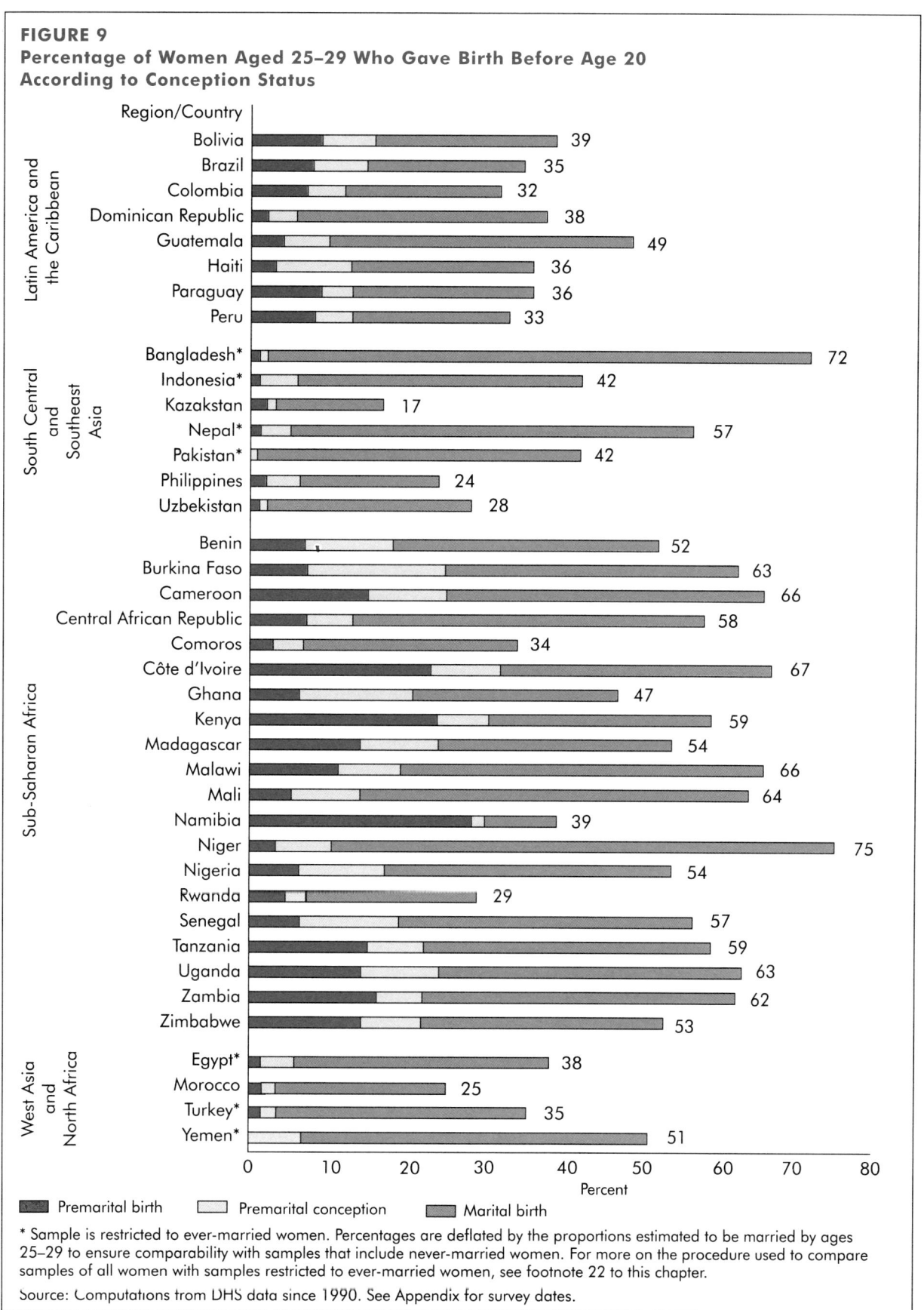

FIGURE 9
Percentage of Women Aged 25–29 Who Gave Birth Before Age 20
According to Conception Status

Region/Country

Latin America and the Caribbean
- Bolivia — 39
- Brazil — 35
- Colombia — 32
- Dominican Republic — 38
- Guatemala — 49
- Haiti — 36
- Paraguay — 36
- Peru — 33

South Central and Southeast Asia
- Bangladesh* — 72
- Indonesia* — 42
- Kazakstan — 17
- Nepal* — 57
- Pakistan* — 42
- Philippines — 24
- Uzbekistan — 28

Sub-Saharan Africa
- Benin — 52
- Burkina Faso — 63
- Cameroon — 66
- Central African Republic — 58
- Comoros — 34
- Côte d'Ivoire — 67
- Ghana — 47
- Kenya — 59
- Madagascar — 54
- Malawi — 66
- Mali — 64
- Namibia — 39
- Niger — 75
- Nigeria — 54
- Rwanda — 29
- Senegal — 57
- Tanzania — 59
- Uganda — 63
- Zambia — 62
- Zimbabwe — 53

West Asia and North Africa
- Egypt* — 38
- Morocco — 25
- Turkey* — 35
- Yemen* — 51

Percent

Legend: Premarital birth / Premarital conception / Marital birth

* Sample is restricted to ever-married women. Percentages are deflated by the proportions estimated to be married by ages 25–29 to ensure comparability with samples that include never-married women. For more on the procedure used to compare samples of all women with samples restricted to ever-married women, see footnote 22 to this chapter.

Source: Computations from DHS data since 1990. See Appendix for survey dates.

TABLE 9A

Percentage of Women Aged 20–39 Who Had a Premarital Birth Before Age 20: Selected Latin American and Caribbean Countries

Country	Age at time of survey			
	20–24	25–29	30–34	35–39
Bolivia	9	10	11	8
Brazil	8	8	6	5
Colombia	9	8	7	7
Dominican Republic	2	1	2	2
Guatemala	4	3	3	6
Paraguay	11	9	10	10
Peru	6	8	7	7

Note: Premarital birth is defined as having occurred a year or more before the date of first marriage reported in the DHS. Marriage is defined to include formal marriage and cohabitation with a male partner.

Source: Computations from DHS data since 1990. See Appendix for survey dates.

in the percentage of women who have had premarital births as adolescents. Among the 11 African countries for which Bledsoe and Cohen computed the percentage of women who had a premarital birth prior to age 20 (Bledsoe and Cohen 1993: Table 2-10) and the seven Latin American countries for which we computed the analogous percentages, only three in Africa—Botswana, Kenya, and Liberia—show a monotonic increase in premarital adolescent childbearing in more recent birth cohorts (see Table 9A for Latin American countries). Even when we expanded our analysis of the Latin American data to include premarital conceptions in addition to births, the percentages were not consistently greater for younger compared to older cohorts (see Table 9B). For example, in Bolivia, 8 percent of women aged 35–39 had a premarital birth before age 20, compared to 9 percent of those aged 20–24; when premarital conceptions are included, the percentages are 18 and 17, respectively. This same pattern prevails in the other countries included in the two tables.[23] What apparently has increased—and will probably increase in the future—is the *percentage* of births to adolescents that are premarital (Bledsoe and Cohen 1993; Singh 1998b).

Early childbearing is believed to have serious consequences for young mothers and their children; however, the literature in this area has been largely confined to health effects.[24] This narrow focus fulfills the

[23] The analysis of changes over time in premarital childbearing is based on comparisons of retrospective accounts from different age cohorts and, as such, is subject to the standard reporting problems that plague survey questions about the more distant past. Furthermore, in societies where consensual unions are common and marriage is a process rather than a well-defined event, designating a behavior as one that took place prior to marriage is problematic.

TABLE 9B

Percentage of Women Aged 20–39 Who Had a Premarital Conception Before Age 20: Selected Latin American and Caribbean Countries

Country	Age at time of survey			
	20–24	25–29	30–34	35–39
Bolivia	17	19	19	18
Brazil	16	17	13	11
Colombia	15	14	13	12
Dominican Republic	4	6	5	10
Guatemala	9	11	10	12
Paraguay	17	15	14	15
Peru	12	14	15	14

Note: Premarital conception is defined as having occurred when the child was born fewer than 7 months after the date of first marriage reported in the DHS. Marriage is defined to include formal marriage and cohabitation with a male partner.

Source: Computations from DHS data since 1990. See Appendix for survey dates

political need to develop strong health-policy rationales for directing services, including controversial family planning services, to adolescents. Indisputably, the health effects of early childbearing are substantial. Childbirth to girls aged 15–19 is associated with a 20 to 200 percent greater chance of dying in pregnancy, as well as increased risk of premature labor, complications during delivery (especially toxemia and cephalo-pelvic disproportion), low birthweight, and infant mortality (Senderowitz 1995). Debate continues over the role of age itself—as opposed to other social, health-seeking, and economic factors—in explaining the negative outcomes of early childbearing. Some health problems of adolescent mothers are clearly age-related, such as vesicovaginal fistulas, which are caused primarily by immature birth canals and prolonged labor (Buvinic and Kurz 1997; McDevitt et al. 1996; Senderowitz 1995). Most reviews of the complex data in this area present compelling arguments to discourage birth before age 18.

The broader life consequences of early childbearing in developing countries have been largely neglected as both a research and policy subject. While the developing-country literature on the social and economic impact of adolescent childbearing is extremely thin, there is evidence that this impact is often negative. The Alan Guttmacher Institute reports that early childbearing "limit[s] educational attainment, restrict[s] the skills young people bring to the work force . . . and reduce[s] their quality of life" (1996: 1). As overall fertility declines and the proportion of

---

[24] For in depth reviews of this literature, see Buvinic and Kurz (1997); McDevitt et al. (1996); Senderowitz (1995).

Only a handful of studies on the social and economic consequences of adolescent fertility have been undertaken in the developing world.

pregnant females who are young rises, interest in the social and economic outcomes of early childbearing may grow.

There is some evidence that negative social and economic effects of early childbearing (both inside and outside of marriage) are increasing, even in places where the proportion of adolescent fertility is not on the rise (Bledsoe and Cohen 1993). When education levels rise along with the demand for skilled labor, those with less schooling and those whose children have less schooling become increasingly marginalized, as has happened in the United States. Early studies in the United States identified adolescent fertility as a precursor to poverty (Furstenberg 1976), although the magnitude and direction of cause and effect are still debated because of the selectivity of teenage mothers—as noted above, they come disproportionately from economically disadvantaged backgrounds—and the inability to adequately control for family characteristics (Furstenberg, Brooks-Gunn, and Morgan 1987; Geronimus and Korenman 1992; Hoffman, Foster, and Furstenberg 1993; Luker 1996).[25]

The absence of data on the key developmental events during adolescence impairs our ability to separate cause from consequence in looking at early childbearing. In sub-Saharan Africa, there is a general belief that, were it not for pregnancy among schoolgirls, educational retention rates for girls would be higher (Ferguson 1988; Meekers and Ahmed 1997; Meekers, Gage, and Zhan 1995). Yet, it is not clear that pregnancy is the principal reason girls drop out of school—indeed, given the large numbers who do drop out, it is implausible that pregnancy is the main cause of this premature departure (Mensch and Lloyd 1998). It may be that school dropout resulting from poor academic performance (or any other reason) makes girls more available for marriage and childbearing, or that parents' and daughters' expectations of early marriage and childbearing reduce girls' commitment to school. The debate surrounding the link between pregnancy and school dropout confirms that we need more than a health and fertility perspective to fully understand girls' experience of adolescence.

Only a handful of studies on the social and economic consequences of adolescent fertility have been undertaken in the developing world. Four of these were supported by a joint Population Council/International

---

[25] While policymakers in the United States have argued that adolescent fertility is always detrimental, some researchers note that in certain socioeconomically disadvantaged populations, "teenage childbearing may not be deviant or 'off time'; rather, a pattern of early fertility may be responsive to social-structural constraints or opportunities. In such a social context, teenage mothers and their children may be supported through multigenerational shared parenting arrangements . . ." (Geronimus, Korenman, and Hillemeier 1994: 586–587).

Center for Research on Women collaborative program in Barbados (Russell-Brown, Engle, and Townsend 1992), Chile (Buvinic 1998), Guatemala (Engle and Smidt 1996), and Mexico (Alatorre and Atkin 1998).[26] Inspired by research on the broad consequences of adolescent childbearing in the United States, the Population Council/ICRW researchers undertook the Latin American/Caribbean studies to generate data on the long-term life circumstances of young mothers, married and unmarried: their family formation patterns, living arrangements, economic welfare, and the locus of financial and emotional responsibility for their children. These studies are far from definitive, particularly given the methodological concerns raised by comparable studies on the consequences of adolescent childbearing in the United States; nevertheless, their results are tantalizing.

The studies, which are based primarily on retrospective data that compare adolescent mothers to later childbearers, found that girls who give birth during adolescence were more likely to be economically disadvantaged later on than girls who delay childbearing. In Mexico, adolescent mothers were six times more likely to live in poverty than women who became mothers as adults (26 percent versus 4.3 percent). In Chile, where the sample separated poor and nonpoor women, adolescent motherhood was associated with lower earnings among poor women only. In both Guatemala and Mexico, poverty indices—housing quality in Guatemala and socioeconomic status in Mexico—were significantly related to adolescent childbearing after controlling for the mother's schooling and economic status as a child.

A noteworthy finding concerned the relationship between adolescent motherhood and subsequent marital status and household structure. In all four countries, adolescent mothers were not less likely than girls without children to marry or find partners. However, in Chile (the only country where this issue was explored in detail), adolescent mothers were significantly less likely than mothers who gave birth as adults to be living with the fathers of their child by the fifth year after birth (after controlling for mothers' education).

These conditions of adolescent mothers' lives in four countries are suggestive of the conditions such girls may face in other developing countries; however, we must gather much more data before we can construct a clear picture of adolescent mothers' lives. To fully understand the immediate effects of early childbearing on adolescent girls, we will need to know: 1) the timing of entry into and exit from school and work rela-

---

[26] For a full review of these studies, see Buvinic (1998).

tive to childbirth; 2) an adolescent mother's relationship with the father of her child at the time of childbirth and subsequent to it; 3) the extent of the father's, or other family members', assistance with child support and child care; and 4) familial attitudes toward an adolescent mother before and after she gives birth. To understand the longer-term consequences of adolescent motherhood, we need longitudinal data from studies that follow adolescent girls for an extended period of time, as well as study designs that enable us to control better for confounding factors that are both a cause and consequence of early childbearing.[27]

Estimates of adolescent childbearing and information about its health consequences are helpful and necessary contributions to our understanding of this phenomenon. However, the systematic neglect of the social and economic context of adolescent childbearing, and the resulting absence of data in this area, have left us with little knowledge about the meaning of childbearing in the lives of adolescent girls and their offspring in developing countries.

---

[27] Using data from the United States, Geronimus and Korenman (1992) compared sisters with different reproductive histories, and Nock (1998) compared brothers in a study of the consequences of premarital fatherhood. These comparisons allowed the researchers to better control for family background.

Chapter 4

Charting a Positive Future for Girls in Developing Countries: An Agenda for Policy, Programs, and Research

In framing adolescent policy, we face a series of obstacles unique to this domain of policy work. At the most basic level, we lack a cultural consensus that adolescence exists as a distinct and important developmental stage for all 10–19-year-old girls and boys, whether or not they are married or have children of their own. In settings where adolescence is acknowledged, it is often not recognized as a period of critical capability-building[1] and heightened vulnerability for girls. Instead, it is commonly viewed as a brief and inconsequential passage for girls—a time of silence, passivity, and devaluation—that ends abruptly at marriage or childbearing. In contrast, adolescent boys are characterized as threatening agents of societal destabilization. Both sets of imagery distort the reality that adolescents are often responsible, capable, and deserving of societal supports and protection. Convincing decisionmakers of this is difficult, however, in the absence of a natural sympathy for adolescents and a clearer picture of their experience. Furthermore, young people do not constitute an organized and vocal constituency with the social and economic power to lobby on their own behalf. Thus, the lack of governmental commitment to adolescents goes largely unchallenged in the political arena. Adolescents do have a growing number of advocates, but they have often promoted a circumscribed, health-centered agenda. This approach, while valuable, neglects the critical components of adolescent girls' experience discussed in Chapter 2. Even the best existing youth policies have not been well or widely implemented. Thus, there is little conceptual or operational precedent for the scope of policy we are calling for. Adolescent policies sensitive to the different needs of girls and boys must be built virtually from the ground up.

---

[1] This useful term was coined by Amartya Sen (1997).

Adolescent girls are virtually invisible in the policy domain.

Because young people lack the power to advocate for themselves, their needs cannot be communicated through normal channels of constituent politics. Though their participation in the formal sector is increasing, their numbers and age limit their influence on workplace policies. Thus, public policy and dialogue are necessary—indeed, primary—mechanisms to improve adolescent lives. Nongovernmental organization (NGO) and private-sector initiatives can certainly catalyze and supplement governmental activity, but there can be no substitute for a public commitment to adolescent girls and boys.

Public policy must set an agenda for adolescent girls that is organized around the distinctive features of their lives: their risk of exploitative living arrangements; confinement to domestic roles and responsibilities; restricted mobility; inadequate and occasionally threatening school experience; unacknowledged work needs and compromising work situations; pressure to marry and begin childbearing early; and limited control over, and knowledge about, their reproductive health and fertility, even (perhaps especially) in the case of married girls. We see four main policy challenges:

- Create a safe, supported passage for girls from ages 10 to 19, recognizing that the second decade of their lives is a period of critical capability-building and heightened vulnerability, which does not end with marriage and childbearing.
- Acknowledge that adolescent girls' lives are often governed by harmful, culturally sanctioned gender rules imposed by males, parents, and other elders and perpetuated at times by girls themselves.
- Expand girls' social participation, schooling, and economic opportunities, understanding that these are basic entitlements and that they frame girls' reproductive behavior.
- Recognize that a large proportion of adolescent girls are already wives and mothers, who need support and investment at least as much as do their unmarried female peers.

Inventing adolescent policy: Making girls visible and valued

At present, adolescent girls are virtually invisible in the policy domain. Viewed along a timeline, policy interest in girls drops off as they leave early childhood and disappears definitively at puberty. Childhood health programs end their concern with girls and boys around the age of 5. Legally mandated schooling typically provides for 6–8 years of education; thus, girls who enroll at ages 5–6 are done with school at the very latest by ages 12–14, roughly coincident with menarche. Girls appear again on the policy screen—if at all—not as unmarried adolescents, but as wives and mothers. Thus, the policy silence around females may extend from prepuberty to the mid-20s, by which time many young women have borne several children.

Adolescent policy must enter into this vacuum of interest. Unlike early women's development efforts—which were able to capitalize on the value attached to women's role as children's caregivers and providers to promote investments in women as individuals—adolescent policy cannot draw on indigenous concepts of girls' inherent value (apart from their future role as wives and mothers). Instead, it must "invent" a value for girls by counteracting customary perceptions of girls (and the legal frameworks that often support them) and by promoting the "novel" concept of girls' rights and capabilities apart from reproduction. Policy must define adolescence as a distinct developmental phase for boys and girls—including those who are married and/or have children—and must attach positive rites of passage, expectations, and opportunities to girls' adolescence.

Recognizing the particularity of girls' adolescence and changing the gender rules

Youth policy and programs, to the extent that they exist, have been weakened by two implicit assumptions: one is that adolescent girls have considerable authority over their lives; the other is that male and female adolescents form a homogenous group with common needs and interests. These misconceptions arise from a failure to recognize or fully appreciate adolescent girls' unique disadvantages and the contrasting experience of girls and boys. A reality-based policy must address both of these dimensions of girls' adolescence.

Youth program documents often overstate adolescents', especially girls', agency over their lives. They sometimes put great faith in the simple provision of information as a means to "help adolescents make better decisions"; but adolescent girls can hardly act on their decisions when they lack control over key resources—indeed, over their lives altogether. An example from Bangladesh illustrates this point. A recent study revealed a four-year gap between married adolescent girls' ideal and actual age at marriage: the girls identified 19 as the ideal age at which to marry, yet their age at marriage averaged 15. The researchers concluded that Bangladeshi girls need to be informed about reproductive processes, sexual intercourse, and the consequences of unsafe sex, early marriage, and early childbirth (expressing the conventional view that reproductive knowledge is the key to changing girls' reproductive behav-

> **Adolescent policy needs a new set of subjects: those who wield power over girls—notably mothers, fathers, boys, and men.**

ior). However, they also acknowledged that parental and cultural pressures compel girls to marry early in Bangladesh; lamented the lack of public support for girls; and noted the "considerable gap. . .between the policies the government has proclaimed and the reality of women's lives" (Haider et al. 1997). This observation underscores the central challenge of adolescent policy: many girls—even those who married at a very young age—know the advantages of later marriage and childbearing, and would have preferred it. What they lack is the means and opportunities to act on this preference.

Adolescent policy must acknowledge that girls are often not responsible for the undesirable outcomes that have drawn attention to them. Denial of schooling, heavy domestic work burdens, lack of opportunity to earn or retain earnings, forced sexual relations, nonconsensual and underage marriage—these widespread conditions reflect and reinforce the constraints on girls' power and autonomy, limiting their ability to control the circumstances of their lives. By extending the boundary of childhood through age 18, the Convention on the Rights of the Child establishes that girls who marry and/or give birth as adolescents remain girls—that is, children—by definition. This should heighten our vigilance concerning the voluntarism of adolescent marriage and sexual relations. It also highlights the need to protect girls' basic right to control their own bodies. At the very least, policies must be built upon the understanding that much of what happens to girls is not an expression of their free will. This public recognition alone would help to validate and potentially empower girls. Ultimately, policy and programs must peel away the many layers of control over girls, challenge discriminatory familial and community norms, and confront male attitudes and behaviors that are damaging to girls.

Recognizing that girls' lives are often controlled by others, adolescent policy needs a new set of subjects: those who wield power over girls notably mothers, fathers, boys, and men. Programs can, and certainly do, strengthen girls as individuals, but the authority and prestige of programs also can be used to change parents' perspectives and behavior. For example, in parts of rural northern Thailand, where an alarming proportion of girls over age 10 reportedly are engaged in some form of commercial sex, the Daughters' Education Program works with parents to channel girls into school. The program sponsors girls' attendance at local secondary or vocational training schools, covering the costs of enrollment fees, uniforms, equipment, activities, and transportation. Girls deemed at risk of being sent into prostitution are selected for the program through extensive interviews of parents, teachers, and girls themselves. Families of participating girls are eligible for special economic programs (Population and Community Development Association 1995). In Egypt, a project in the Maqattam settlement (a garbage-collecting community on the outskirts of Cairo) offers 500 pounds to girls who delay marriage to age 18. This cash gift gives girls leverage with parents; and project organizers use their strong community base to gather sensitive information about hidden subjects, such as girls' real age at marriage and whether or not their marriage is voluntary.

Adolescent policy must differentiate the particular conditions of adolescent girls' and boys' lives. Only girls get pregnant; a far greater proportion of girls marry as adolescents; and girls appear to be more frequent targets of sexual abuse. As it stands, however, official policy holds girls accountable for outcomes, such as pregnancy, that are equally, if not entirely, the result of boys' or men's actions. When a girl becomes pregnant, she is typically forced to leave school, while the boy or man who impregnated her not only escapes censure but is almost never identified.

Adolescent programs sometimes foster the notion that adolescents constitute a cohesive group, thereby giving more attention to intergenerational tensions than to gender conflicts. In reality, adolescent girls and their male companions often have conflicting interests. The organizers of *Gente Joven*, an innovative reproductive health program in Mexico, learned this through first-hand experience. They developed a short educational film about adolescent pregnancy, in which a romance between an adolescent boy and girl culminates in pregnancy, with the couple deciding to run off together to escape their insensitive families. When this story line was presented to young people, boys and girls alike challenged its portrayal of reality. They asserted that, even when a boy and girl are greatly in love, the boy is likely to abandon the girl, sometimes abruptly, if she becomes pregnant. The program organizers subsequently rewrote the script to include a more realistic ending (Marques 1993).

An example from a soccer league for boys and girls in Kenya further illustrates this issue. Girls' childcare responsibilities had impeded their participation in the league, requiring the provision of tents for childcare along the sidelines of playing fields. The boys wanted to purchase impressive heavy tents, ignoring the fact that the girls wished to carry and erect the tents on their own. In a "gender training" session, the girls were given a public voice and were allowed to reject "collective" decisions made by the boys. In this session, the girls argued successfully for the purchase of lighter tents (Brady 1997).

> **Because the health and family planning communities have generated most of the interest in adolescence, much adolescent policy remains centered in the health sector.**

Moving adolescent policy beyond reproductive health

Adolescent fertility has been characterized as a reproductive health problem. This view is not entirely inaccurate, but it is incomplete. Negative health outcomes are, indeed, a possible consequence of adolescent fertility (see "Childbearing" in Chapter 3). What has been largely overlooked is that girls in most cultures can achieve social mobility and economic security only (if at all) through the medium of their sexuality and fertility. Very likely, the best means to avert adolescent pregnancy (if this remains a key policy objective) is by offering girls alternative sources of social status and productive activity.

Because the health and family planning communities have generated most of the interest in adolescence, much adolescent policy remains centered in the health sector. Innovative development programs for women have revealed strong links between women's exercise of their reproductive rights and their acquisition of social and economic power. Girls' education is known to promote later marriage, and income-earning work may do so as well—as suggested, for example, by the persuasive study of later marriage among garment-factory workers in Bangladesh (Amin et al. 1998). Thus, we must move beyond the traditional purview of the family planning establishment and institute measures other than health interventions to reduce adolescent fertility. This will require advocacy and budgetary resources for social and economic investments outside the health sector.

At present, however, the spectrum of adolescent programs remains restricted. The International Center for Research on Women queried the leaders of well-regarded, often multipurpose organizations serving youth in Africa, Asia, and Latin America to determine what they consider the most crucial issues for young people today. In Africa, 40 percent of the respondents identified unemployment and access to resources; in Asia, 40 percent cited education. Yet only 4 percent of the programs sponsored by these organizations dealt with unemployment and income generation, and only 10 percent dealt with education (Peplinsky 1994).

It is past time to develop a multisectoral adolescent policy. We need diverse initiatives that improve the conditions of girls' lives, not only in the realm of reproductive health, but also in the areas of work, sports, and schooling. Fortunately, we do not have to begin at ground zero; some remarkable, multipurpose youth projects run by nongovernmental organizations (NGOs) are already underway.[2]

Expanding girls' economic options should be a priority. We ought to investigate whether adolescent girls could be included in some of the innovative development programs for women. The bold experiments of the last 20 years that have increased women's economic prospects in nontraditional ways have limited participation to married and socially senior women. Microenterprise, savings, and credit schemes that have begun to reconfigure married women's status still typically exclude unmarried females, even those of the same age as their married peers. This resistance may reflect a belief that unmarried adolescent girls lack skills, collateral, and effective social power, are unreliable, and have little experience in cooperative enterprises. This is reminiscent of the bias that initially excluded women from traditionally male-centered development schemes; yet, experience has demonstrated that women are far better credit risks than men, on average, and poor women are especially good risks (Hussain 1986). Perhaps the same will prove to be the case for adolescent girls.

Girls' current work participation, increased time availability for wage labor, and need for income argue for increasing their participation in appropriately scaled productivity schemes. Not only are girls likely to benefit economically from inclusion in these schemes, they are also bound to benefit from participation in the female solidarity groups that work as teams in the most successful enterprises. Although the examples are few, there is some evidence—for example, from the Maqattam project and from the Centre for Mass Education in Science–Grameen Bank program (see footnote 2)—that girls as young as 12 and 13 may eagerly participate in income-generating programs that allow them time to grow up and acquire more power in their families (Assaad and Bruce 1997; Centre for Mass Education in Science 1993). In the United States, economic components are being added to programs initiated to reduce teen pregnancy, in which conventional life-skills training and health education approaches have yielded insufficient results.[3]

Including younger females in economic programs for women may help to resolve a continuing debate over the role of these programs in fertility decline. Analysts agree that they serve as an excellent base for the provision of modern contraceptive services. However, most of these programs engage women who have, or have nearly, attained their desired

---

[2] Innovative programs for adolescent girls are profiled in an unpublished Population Council document (1996). These programs include, for example, the Adolescent Girls' Program of the Centre for Mass Education in Science and Grameen Bank in Bangladesh, which offers unmarried girls aged 13–19 access to education, job training, microenterprise and credit opportunities, health education, and physical exercise.

[3] The Georgia Initiative on Teen Pregnancy (founded in 1996) includes an economic component. The Entrepreneurial Development Institute Program in Washington, DC (founded in 1991) assists disadvantaged youths aged 17–21 in developing their own small businesses, using loans and other resources.

Not only do girls need access to microenterprise, savings, and credit programs, they also need opportunities for wage-earning work outside the home in the formal sector.

family size; thus, the programs' impact on fertility remains unclear. Opening up economic schemes to unmarried or recently married adolescent girls, and following their progress, could help to clarify the links between women's economic security, desired fertility levels, and attainment of their reproductive goals.[4]

Not only do girls need access to microenterprise, savings, and credit programs, they also need opportunities for wage-earning work outside the home in the formal sector. Dixon-Mueller recognized the potential demographic benefits of such work two decades ago, as demonstrated by her prescient call for efforts to "recruit unmarried girls and young married women in their early childbearing years [for employment outside the home] so that their new status can have a maximum potential impact on delaying marriage, delaying their first birth, and spacing and limiting additional births" (1978: 132). One of the earliest efforts to engage young females in formal-sector work was undertaken in 1974 by the Egyptian Supreme Council of Family Planning. Fueled by the finding that women's agricultural work may in some cases sustain high fertility (Bindary, Baxter, and Hollingsworth 1973), the council launched an innovative and much-publicized project to employ young females (many of them married) in a factory in Tahrir, a desert reclamation site (Bruce 1976). While many observers were intrigued by this effort to employ girls in the formal sector, this strategy has never been promoted on a large scale nor seriously considered as a policy option in any country. Nevertheless, an increasing number of females, many of them young and unmarried, are working in textile factories in parts of Asia, as well as in Costa Rica and Mauritius, as noted in Chapter 2 (Amin et al. 1998; Anker 1998; Wolf 1992). This natural experiment in female employment could be harnessed to improve girls' social position, economic prospects, and reproductive wellbeing. In addition to ensuring that girls are protected by safe and fair labor practices (a matter of much international concern at the moment), programs linked to work sites could provide girls with life-skills training, health information, sports activities, and means to manage their income through savings and credit mechanisms.

Adolescent girls need opportunities to empower themselves physically as well as economically. Programs for younger girls sometimes include dance, play, and other leisure activities; but programs for girls of all ages rarely include physically vigorous outdoor sports (though many countries have ministries of youth and sports). Involving girls in sports can

---

[4] These linkages were explored in a 1997 seminar, "Measuring the Impact of Microcredit Programs on Fertility," organized by Sajeda Amin at the Population Council.

foster their self-confidence, self-defense skills, and pride in their bodies' physical powers apart from reproduction, with logical links to reproductive health (Brady 1998). Sports and other group activities offer a power base outside the family, where mentoring and peer support can be provided. Recognizing the benefits of sports for personal growth, the Dutch government has established a mechanism to fund sports initiatives in developing countries (Netherlands Ministry of Foreign Affairs and Netherlands Ministry of Health, Welfare, and Sport 1998).

Creating a distinct "space for girls"—whether the entry point is work, sports, or other social activities—would benefit them on many levels. Such spaces would serve as zones of relative safety for girls and contexts in which they could develop identities outside of their relationships with parents and males. They would also provide venues in which information about reproductive health, life skills, and other vital subjects can be offered through ongoing, interactive dialogue.

Education is the most obvious public lever to change girls' situation. Any adolescent policy that is intelligently embedded in a national development strategy will recognize that girls' education is "the most influential investment" (Summers 1992). Beyond its measurable demographic and economic returns to society, schooling offers girls something that cannot be taken away from them: awareness of their own abilities and an experience of the world outside their homes.

Expanding girls' education is a keystone of a broadly conceived population policy because it has the potential simultaneously to raise the age of childbearing, reduce desired family size, and empower females with the knowledge and social authority to space and limit childbearing and to invest in their children. However, education will not transform girls' futures unless its content is carefully constructed. Girls need academic and vocational training that equips them with skills that are marketable within their country's current economy—and not merely skills needed for the lowest-paying, sex-segregated jobs. Girls are not well served by more years of schooling that fail to increase their livelihood prospects. Certainly more girls need more education—but, above all, they need better-quality and more-relevant education.

Almost all governments have publicly assigned a high value to schooling as a means to achieve democratization, social change, and economic development. Those wishing to improve girls' education can make use of existing education policy, infrastructure, and teacher training programs, however flawed they may be. Pledges to increase government spending in the education sector are welcome, but blanket increases may be less beneficial than wisely targeted investments in the educational resources that help girls the most. Decisionmakers will need sound information to identify these resources. Are funds better spent at the primary, secondary, or tertiary level? What kind of vocational training should girls receive? Are they better educated in single-sex or coeducational classrooms? What teaching methods are most effective for them? Where are the critical links between education and formal-sector work? These kinds of questions must be answered in every setting.

Advances in girls' education need not await major changes in formal education systems. Creative initiatives, some of them large-scale, are already underway in some developing countries. These include nonformal educational opportunities that feed into formal school systems, economic incentives for parents to educate their daughters, and programs to involve parents and communities in decisions regarding girls' education, such as one now operating in Pakistan (Sathar 1998). Examples of incentive programs include the Daughters' Education Program in northern Thailand (described earlier) and a secondary-school scholarship program in Bangladesh, which covers the cost of girls' school fees, books, and uniforms. The Bangladesh program also offers a small monthly stipend valued at US$1–2, which is deposited into a bank account belonging to the girl (Amin and Sedgh 1998). The Bangladesh Rural Advancement Committee runs a notable program that has created more than 30,000 schools providing nonformal primary education to nearly one million children—70 percent of them girls (by design)—aged 6–14. These schools have maintained exceptionally high attendance rates; most impressively, 90 percent of the graduates have gained admission to class four in the public school system (Ahmed et al. 1993). The CamFed Zimbabwe Project works with groups of girls and their families to help the girls complete secondary school in a poor district with stark gender imbalances in school enrollment (despite strong governmental endorsement of girls' education). In the first five years of the program (1991–96), not one family turned down the offer of support for a daughter's education (Cotton 1997).

Education is often characterized as an intervention that takes generations to bear returns; but some of the initiatives described above have already yielded positive short-term results. For example, girls' school enrollment in Bangladesh and Pakistan rose in response to the scholarship and parent/community involvement programs (Amin and Sedgh 1998; Arends-Kuenning, Sedgh, and Amin 1998; Herz et al. 1991). The scholarship program in Bangladesh had an immediate and significant impact on girls' age at marriage in villages studied by Amin and Sedgh (1998): between 1992 and 1995, the proportion of married 13–15-year-olds dropped from 29 to 14 percent, and the proportion of married 16–19-year-olds fell from 72 to 64 percent in these villages. It is notable that efforts to increase girls' school attendance have been well received in diverse settings in which resistance to girls' schooling was thought to be substantial. Parents and communities may be ready to educate girls if the social and economic costs of doing so are even slightly reduced.

There are tactical reasons to move adolescent policy and programs away from their tight association with sexuality and fertility. This link may reinforce the very bias that renders girls vulnerable—namely the tendency to view them as sex and fertility objects. Controversies over family-life education and the offering of contraceptive services to young people may also distort the public perception of adolescence by focusing exclusive (and negative) attention on its sexual dimension. The moral objections of parents and communities to adolescent programs may lessen if these programs were framed as opportunities for work, sports, and education. It is thus more realistic, fairer to girls, and probably politically expedient to frame adolescent policy in a broad development context.

Supporting girls through sexual initiation, pregnancy, and marriage

Girls' promise and vulnerability—indeed, their adolescence—do not end when their sexual, reproductive, and/or married lives begin. Adolescent programs may view girls who have suffered one or more negative outcomes—for example, unplanned pregnancy or involuntary marriage—as "failures." The underlying assumption is that a pregnant or married girl's future is unalterably scripted; thus, energy should be turned to "uninitiated" girls. But a large fraction of adolescent girls are sexually active, pregnant, and/or married, and still have much of their lives ahead of them. The policy challenge is to develop a series of supports tailored to specific ages and situations (Hughes and McCauley 1998), so that adolescence can be a period of growth and achievement for all girls, regardless of their sexual, reproductive, or marital status.

Most programs aiming to change adolescents' reproductive behavior dispense information to the unmarried. These programs usually focus narrowly on reproductive physiology and methods to avoid pregnancy and (to a lesser extent) on sexually transmitted infections. Some progressive programs have expanded their range of topics to include sexual pleasure, gender equality, partner communication, and a broader spectrum of reproductive health issues (Barker and Loewenstein 1996; Faiz, Banu, and Sharma 1996).

> Girls' promise and vulnerability do not end when their sexual, reproductive, and/or married lives begin.

Governments and NGOs have taken some measures to encourage girls to marry later, ranging from information dissemination campaigns to more comprehensive strategies. In Indonesia in the 1980s, Pathfinder Fund supported a network of community-based organizations to publicize (through mosques, for example) the increase in the legal age at marriage from 14 to 16 for girls, and from 16 to 19 for boys. In India, a far more ambitious, better-organized, and still unfolding effort is underway to increase the value placed on girls, and thereby indirectly increase their age at marriage. The governments of several large Indian states (Haryana, Karnataka, and Rajasthan) have set aside small sums of money for girls at birth as a means to ensure their survival, encourage gender equality, and balance skewed sex ratios. Between the ages of 18 and 21, girls (married or not) are eligible to collect respectable sums (for example, in Haryana State, girls collect 25,000 rupees at age 18). This economic scheme is supplemented by supports for girls' education in a broad design to delay marriage. It is posited that even—and, perhaps, especially—girls bound in traditional dowry systems (despite its being outlawed in many places) will be motivated to defer marriage until receipt of this money (Greene 1997). These impressive efforts may lead to significant changes in girls' experience and, thus, should be studied closely.

Unmarried girls who are pregnant or have children have been the subject of several small-scale, but often vigorous programs in Latin America and sub-Saharan Africa. Well-documented experiments in Botswana, Jamaica, and Tanzania, for example, offer living quarters for pregnant adolescents and counseling for mothers and the fathers of their children. They also encourage changes in school-leaving and return-to-school policies for these girls (Cooper, Paxman, and Mwateba 1988; International Youth Foundation 1992; McNeil et al. 1983).

The belief in young people's "resilience" (Resnick et al. 1997) underlies efforts to work with girls who are already sexually initiated or pregnant; however, there is little faith in the resilience of married girls.[5] These girls not only comprise a large group of adolescents, they are also very much in need of support. Yet, married and soon-to-be-married girls and their partners have been neglected by most informational programs. Some governments have made passing efforts to inform couples about reproductive health issues when they register to marry or apply for a

---

[5] The concept of "resilience" suggests that youth who have engaged in a "risky" behavior—unsafe sex, drug use, a nonmarital pregnancy—can respond to appropriate support, information, and services and are resilient enough to have productive, safer lives in the future.

marriage license, by offering pamphlets and a lecture at some point in the official process. In an effort to delay first birth after marriage, the government of Bangladesh has, in recent years, used media messages to exhort newly married couples to practice contraception. In general, however, married and soon-to-be-married adolescents lack critical information about, and need more opportunities to discuss, sexuality, male/female relationships, parenting, and other subjects related to their unfolding sexual and reproductive lives—notably, the life-transforming experience of first birth.

Married girls need active support during the rapid, and sometimes traumatic, transitions of early married life. Many of these girls face their first birth triply disadvantaged by their age, gender, and subservient position as young wives in often extended families.[6] Primiparous females have special needs for information and support, which they often fail to receive.[7] The few formal services for young mothers generally overlook their social needs and the significance of a first birth. In reporting on the impact of a first birth in the United States, Presser observes: "Having a first birth means becoming a mother unless the child dies or is given up for adoption. The permanence of motherhood makes it the most critical of all role transitions" (1971: 336).

The role of male partners in supporting young wives during early marriage, pregnancy, and first birth has not been adequately explored. Efforts to engage husbands and fathers in the early stages of family formation are rare and poorly documented. Reproductive health programs have generally excluded men, although male involvement is increasingly encouraged in fertility-regulation services. Maternal/child health, pregnancy-support, delivery, and postpartum services make little provision for male participation, and often explicitly exclude fathers. Studies suggest that including men in these arenas would benefit mothers, fathers, and children alike. A comprehensive postpartum program in Turkey found, for example, that when fathers were included in the program, postpartum use of contraceptives and compliance with maternal and infant health checkups increased (Molzan-Turan 1996). In Nicaragua—where a substantial proportion of births are to unmarried women, and a high percentage of households with children are headed only by mothers—one exploratory program will try to promote fathers'

Many married girls face their first birth triply disadvantaged by their age, gender, and subservient position as young wives in often extended families.

---

[6] For example, Das Gupta remarks upon "the convergence of low autonomy due to youth as well as sex among young women in South Asia" (1996: 213).

[7] Janet Molzan-Turan and associates at the Istanbul University Institute of Child Health are focusing a new research program on how best to support young, married females who are pregnant with their first child (Molzan-Turan 1997).

practical and emotional support for new mothers and involvement with their children by including them in pregnancy and postpartum care (Engle and Loftin 1997).

In many cultures, newly married couples face inexorable pressure to produce a child as soon as possible. In these settings, programmatic efforts to delay the first birth are likely to meet more resistance than are efforts to support couples during the first pregnancy and first birth. Such programs could yield important, long-term returns. Patterns established during the first pregnancy tend to become habits throughout a reproductive lifetime. Involving young fathers as well as mothers in first-birth programs could lay the foundation for more gender equity and greater male investment in children. Focusing on this critical phase in the lifecycle might empower the youngest mothers and their partners to adopt longer spacing intervals and appropriate infant/child health and reproductive health practices. For poor women, who generally have few points of contact with government and community services, first-pregnancy/first-birth interventions could open up a formal channel of referral to continuing education, livelihood-skills training, leadership opportunities, and so forth.

Policymakers must abandon the traditional view that females' lives as individuals end with marriage and/or motherhood. Adolescent girls should be given every opportunity to postpone marriage and pregnancy, but those who do marry and/or have children should be supported and not deprived of further development.

Research priorities: Widening the lens and deepening the analysis

The gaps and biases in information on developing-country adolescents reflect two factors: the low interest in adolescents on the part of the development community and the agenda of the population and family planning field, which has sponsored much of the research in this area and has defined the field of inquiry. According to critiques of twentieth-century demography, the close alliance between the family planning establishment and those conducting population research has led to the neglect of the role of social setting and individual motivation in reproductive behavior (Demeny 1988; Greenhalgh 1996). As a result, policies to control adolescent fertility sometimes have taken on the coloration of a junior family planning agenda. Fortunately, this is beginning to change.

Our advice is to accelerate radically all efforts to broaden the types of data collected on adolescents and to contextualize their experience. We recommend that researchers resist the temptation to draw conclusions about adolescents' lives from data on 5-year or 10-year cohorts of young people. While conflating the experience of 25–29-year-olds may be appropriate, the density of transitions during adolescence requires a more refined picture. Thus, we recommend that researchers gather data on smaller—possibly even single-year—cohorts of adolescents in developing countries. We urge them to give more attention to the youngest adolescents and to separate the experiences of girls and boys, as well as the meaning they attach to these experiences. We advocate obtaining more data on adolescents in the following areas:

- their time use
- their living arrangements
- whether and by whom they are offered protection and economic support
- where they spend time, with whom they affiliate, and how they participate in community life
- their public rites of passage
- their school experience—including the regularity of their attendance, the content of their lessons, the age appropriateness of their grade level, the risks they face at school, and the attitudes conveyed by their teachers and teaching materials
- their leisure activities
- their mobility
- their overall health
- their productive work and livelihood prospects

The relative priority of these subjects will vary in different settings. However, all research needs to distinguish the gender- and age-based dimensions of adolescent experience. Encrypted in the ten largely unexplored years of adolescence are the lifetime choices of girls and boys.

The social and economic lives of adolescents have been blacked out and need to be illuminated. Curiously, adolescent fertility research has neglected what one would have thought would be a key subject: married adolescents, the vast majority of whom are female, who may constitute the largest pool of sexually active adolescents. As indicated earlier, we know few details of their passage into marriage; the age and power differentials and communication patterns between married adolescents and their spouses; the feelings and information brought to adolescent marriage; first sexual relations, pregnancy, and birth; and newly married couples' social affiliations, livelihood strategies, and educational needs. We lack a significant body of research in developing countries on the social and economic consequences of early childbearing, inside or outside of marriage. Such data would greatly strengthen the arguments both against early childbearing and in favor of desirable policies outside

> **Research needs to distinguish the gender- and age-based dimensions of adolescent experience.**

the health sector that help to delay childbearing—namely, those promoting education and livelihood opportunities for girls.

Investing in the largest generation of girls ever

A confluence of factors at the end of this century and the beginning of the next could finally render investments in adolescents a centerpiece of economic development. The sheer number of adolescents in most countries, even where the proportion of youth is falling, is stunning. Both high- and low-fertility societies have good reason to intensify investments in adolescents as a means to ensure societal survival. Where fertility is low and young people comprise a shrinking proportion of the population, there are concerns about the dependency burden of an aging population. Plausibly, the best way to ensure a strong tax base and the survival of social security systems is to invest sufficiently in young people for them to become a productive, long-term workforce capable of generating the revenues to fund the entitlements of the elderly as well as the young. For different reasons, the same argument can be made in countries that are still concerned about high, if declining, fertility. Intergenerational concerns are not absent in these societies; for example, the Malawi Youth Strategy has called for lowering the retirement age to make way for a wave of youth employment (Government of Malawi 1995). Solutions to resource and population problems in high-fertility societies also lie in investments in young people. Such investments, particularly in education, are among the most effective ways to delay childbearing, which by itself—even without declines in family size—will reduce population growth. Social investments in youth also create the conditions for voluntary fertility decline, increased productivity, and higher and more equally distributed incomes (Birdsall 1995). In sum, regardless of where you sit, building the human capability of adolescents appears to be an inescapably good idea.

Thoughtful adolescent policy would be particularly ill-served by a single-sector approach (Commonwealth Secretariat 1990; Ferguson 1996). Yet, it would be naïve to assume that multisectoral adolescent policies will not face many of the barriers that have impeded cross-sectoral cooperation in other areas (Population Council and Overseas Development Council 1998). Cooperation is often thwarted by the guild mentality of bureaucracies that wish to make proprietary claims to a problem and the resources devoted to solving it. There is a risk that ministries of health will serve as the exclusive seat of adolescent policy. Ministries of education, employment, labor, youth, community development, and sports must all contribute to implementing not just a multisectoral health agenda, but rather a broadly cast program.

Delivering services to adolescents must also rely on greatly expanded engagement by NGOs. Much has been said at international conferences about the value of these organizations, and their numbers are increasing (Mathews 1997). Their advantages over government lie in their multiplicity, maneuverability, and ability to gain the trust and reflect the perspectives of less powerful groups, such as women and youth. Reaching adolescent girls requires working from a community base and responding dynamically to interconnected needs. NGOs are adept at reaching adolescents through diverse entry points and, having entered through one door (say, an economic one), moving laterally to offer related services. Few successful adolescent programs remain single-purpose operations; the same is true of NGOs.

As donors are encouraged to direct more resources to adolescents, they will have to find avenues apart from standard governmental structures through which to reach them. NGOs are one such avenue, but rarely can an NGO effectively absorb large revenues. One solution is to establish country-level umbrella mechanisms, such as youth foundations and other entities, that can receive large funding blocks from governments and bilateral/multilateral donors, and can then "retail" these funds in the form of much smaller grants to community-based groups.[8]

In a world of increasingly porous boundaries and political complexity, global thinkers are puzzled, looking for points of reference and leverage to understand and shape the future. They classify countries in regional or cultural power blocs; identify power elites and influential individuals; and rank transnational corporations by size. Appearing on none of these power lists is one of the potentially most influential figures in the developing world: the 12-year-old girl. There are now 50 million of these girls and there will continue to be at least that many every year for the next three decades (United Nations 1997). In the next few years, this 12-year-old girl will either abandon or continue her schooling, be pushed into marriage and childbearing or develop a sense of proud ownership of her physical self and make independent decisions about her lifetime partner. She will either struggle in poverty or find a socially productive livelihood, submit to a faceless life or thrive as an individual, making her contribution to the world. As her future is reconfigured, so is ours.

---

[8] The International Youth Foundation and Synergos Institute have helped to establish such mechanisms for providing financial and technical resources to NGOs, including those serving youth.

Dates of Demographic and Health Surveys Used in This Study

Region/Country	Year
Latin America and the Caribbean	
Bolivia	1993–94
Brazil	1996
Colombia	1995
Dominican Republic	1991
Guatemala	1995
Haiti	1994–95
Paraguay	1990
Peru	1991
South Central and Southeast Asia	
Bangladesh	1994
Indonesia	1994
Kazakstan	1995
Nepal	1996
Pakistan	1991
Philippines	1993
Uzbekistan	1996
Sub-Saharan Africa	
Benin	1996
Burkina Faso	1993
Cameroon	1991
Central African Republic	1994–95
Comoros	1996
Côte d'Ivoire	1994
Ghana	1993
Kenya	1993
Madagascar	1992
Malawi	1996
Mali	1995–96
Namibia	1992
Niger	1992
Nigeria	1990
Rwanda	1992
Senegal	1992
Tanzania	1994
Uganda	1995
Zambia	1992
Zimbabwe	1994
West Asia and North Africa	
Egypt	1992
Morocco	1992
Turkey	1993
Yemen	1991–92

Note: These are the 39 DHS surveys since 1990 for which data were available in mid-1998.

References

Abdalla, Raqiya Haji Dualeh. 1982. *Sisters in Affliction: Circumcision and Infibulation of Women in Africa*. London: Zed Press.

Ahmed, Manzoor et al. 1993. *Primary Education for All: Learning from the BRAC Experience: A Case Study*. Washington, DC: Project ABEL, The Academy for Educational Research.

Ainsworth, Martha. 1996. "Economic aspects of child fostering in Côte d'Ivoire," *Research in Population Economics* 8: 25–62.

Ainsworth, Martha, Kathleen Beegle, and Andrew Nyamete. 1996. "The impact of women's schooling on fertility and contraceptive use: A study of fourteen sub-Saharan African communities," *World Bank Economic Review* 10, no. 1: 85–122.

Ajayi, Ayo A., Leah T. Marangu, Janice Miller, and John M. Paxman. 1991. "Adolescent sexuality and fertility in Kenya: A survey of knowledge, perceptions, and practices," *Studies in Family Planning* 22, no. 4: 205–216.

Ajayi, Ayo et al. 1997. *Schooling and the Experience of Adolescents in Kenya*. Nairobi: Population Council and the Government of Kenya Ministry of Education.

Alan Guttmacher Institute. 1996. *Risks and Realities of Early Childbearing Worldwide*. New York.

———. 1998. *Into a New World: Young Women's Sexual and Reproductive Lives*. New York.

Alatorre Rico, Javier and Lucille C. Atkin. 1998. "De abuela a madre, de madre a hijas: Repetición intergeneracional del embarazo adolescente y la pobreza" (From grandmother to mother, from mother to children: Intergenerational repetition of adolescent pregnancy and poverty), in Beatriz Schmukler (ed.), *Transformaciones de la Familia en América Latina y el Caribe: Una Perspectiva de Género* (*Transformation in Families: Changes in Gender Relations and the Situation of Children in Latin America*). Mexico City: Population Council and Editores Asociados Mexicanos, pp. 419–450.

Alexander, K. C. 1991. "Pattern of utilization of time in rural households in areas with different levels of economic development," *Man in India* 71, no. 1: 305–329.

Amazigo, Uche, Nancy Silva, Joan Kaufman, and Daniel S. Obikeze. 1997. "Sexual activity and contraceptive knowledge and use among in-school adolescents in Nigeria," *International Family Planning Perspectives* 23, no. 1: 28–33.

Amin, Sajeda. 1996. "Female education and fertility in Bangladesh: The influence of marriage and the family," in Roger Jeffery and Alaka M. Basu (eds.), *Girls' Schooling, Women's Autonomy and Fertility Change in South Asia*. New Delhi: Sage Publications, pp. 184–204.

———. 1998. Personal communication.

Amin, Sajeda and Mead Cain. 1997. "The rise of dowry in Bangladesh," in Gavin W. Jones et al. (eds.), *The Continuing Demographic Transition*. Oxford: Clarendon Press, pp. 290–306.

Amin, Sajeda, Ian Diamond, Ruchira T. Naved, and Margaret Newby. 1998. "Transition to adulthood of female garment-factory workers in Bangladesh," *Studies in Family Planning* 29, no. 2: 185–200.

Amin, Sajeda and Cynthia B. Lloyd. Forthcoming. "Women's lives and rapid fertility decline: Some lessons from Bangladesh and Egypt," Policy Research Division Working Paper. New York: Population Council.

Amin, Sajeda and Gilda Sedgh. 1998. "Incentive schemes for school attendance in rural Bangladesh," Policy Research Division Working Paper no. 106. New York: Population Council.

Anderson-Levitt, Kathryn M., Marianne Bloch, and Aminata M. Soumaré. 1998. "Inside classrooms in Guinea: Girls' experiences," in Marianne Bloch, Josephine A. Beoku-Betts, and B. Robert Tabachnick (eds.), *Women and Education in Sub-Saharan Africa: Powers, Opportunities, and Constraints*. Boulder, CO: Lynne Rienner Publishers, pp. 99–130.

Anker, Richard. 1998. *Gender and Jobs: Sex Segregation of Occupations in the World*. Geneva: International Labour Office.

Appfel-Marglin, Frederique. 1996. "Of Pirs and Pandits: Tradition of Hindu-Muslim cultural commonalities in Orissa," *Manushi* no. 91: 17–26.

Arends-Kuenning, Mary, Gilda Sedgh, and Sajeda Amin. 1998. "Effects of schooling incentive programs on household time allocation," paper presented at the Annual Meeting of the Population Association of America, 2–4 April, Chicago.

Assaad, Marie and Judith Bruce. 1997. "Empowering the next generation: Girls of the Maqattam garbage settlement," *SEEDS* no. 19. New York: Population Council.

Aziz, K. M. Ashraful. 1989. "Daughters and sons in rural Bangladesh: Gender creation from birth to adolescence," in Maithreyi Krishnaraj and Karuna Chanana (eds.), *Gender and the Household Domain: Social and Cultural Dimensions*. New Delhi: Sage Publications, pp. 55–73.

Bagasao, Teresita Marie P. 1992. "Sex, tourism, street children, and HIV in the Philippines: Lessening risks in the poverty trap," *World AIDS* no. 20: 7.

Balk, Deborah, Grace Cruz, and Tim Brown. 1997. "HIV/AIDS risk in the Philippines: Focus on adolescents and young adults," East-West Center Working Papers in Population no. 93. Honolulu.

Barker, Gary and Felicia Knaul. 1992. "Three times exploited, three times empowered: The urban adolescent woman in difficult circumstances," final draft of a report to the Urban Section of the United Nations Children's Fund (UNICEF), 28 October.

Barker, Gary and Irene Loewenstein. 1996. "Where the boys are: Promoting greater male involvement in sexuality education: Conclusions from qualitative research in Rio de Janeiro, Brazil," report prepared for the Centro de Educação Sexual, Rio de Janeiro.

Barnes-Josiah, Debora and Antoine Augustin. 1995. "Secular trend in the age at menarche in Haiti," *American Journal of Human Biology* 7, no. 3: 357–362.

Bastos, A. V., L. Morris, and S. R. Fernandes. 1989. *Saúde e Educação Sexual do Jovem: Um Estudo en Salvador, Brasil*. Salvador, Brazil: Universidade Federal de Bahia.

Bindary, Aziz, Collin B. Baxter, and T. H. Hollingsworth. 1973. "Urban-rural differences with the relationship between women's employment and fertility: A preliminary study," *Journal of Biosocial Science* 5, no. 2: 159–167.

Birdsall, Nancy. 1995. "Inequality and growth reconsidered: Lessons from east Africa," *The World Bank Economic Review* 9, no. 3: 477–508.

Blanc, Ann K. and Ann A. Way. 1998. "Sexual behavior and contraceptive knowledge and use among adolescents in developing countries," *Studies in Family Planning* 29, no. 2: 106–116.

Bledsoe, Caroline H. 1990. "School fees and the marriage process for Mende girls in Sierra Leone," in Peggy Reeves Sanday and Ruth Gallagher Goodenough (eds.), *New Directions in the Anthropology of Gender*. Philadelphia: University of Pennsylvania, pp. 283–309.

———. 1996. Personal communication.

Bledsoe, Caroline H. and Barney Cohen. 1993. *Social Dynamics of Adolescent Fertility in Sub-Saharan Africa*. Washington, DC: National Academy Press.

Bledsoe, Caroline H. and Uche Isiugo-Abanihe. 1989. "Strategies of child-fosterage among Mende grannies in Sierra Leone," in Ron J. Lesthaeghe (ed.), *Reproduction and Social Organization in Sub-Saharan Africa*. Berkeley: University of California Press, pp. 442–474.

Bongaarts, John. 1994. "Population policy options in the developing world," *Science* 263, no. 5148: 771–776.

———. 1998. Personal communication.

Bongaarts, John and Barney Cohen. 1998. "Introduction and overview," *Studies in Family Planning* 29, no. 2: 99–105.

Boohene, Esther et al. 1991. "Fertility and contraceptive use among young adults in Harare, Zimbabwe," *Studies in Family Planning* 22, no. 4: 264–271.

Borongo, Longin R. et al. 1992. "The epidemiology of HIV-1 infection in urban areas, roadside settlements, and rural villages in Mwanza, Tanzania," *AIDS* 6, no. 12: 1521–1528.

Bos, Eduard, My T. Vu, Ernest Massiah, and Rodolfo A. Bulatao. 1994. *World Population Projections 1994–95 Edition: Estimates and Projections with Related Demographic Statistics*. Baltimore: Johns Hopkins University Press.

Bouis, Howarth E. 1996. Personal communication.

Bouis, Howarth E., Marilou Palabrica-Costello, Orville Solon, and Azucena B. Limbo. 1994. "Understanding gender-differentiated constraints to Philippine farm household investments in adolescents: Implications for their nutritional status," Nutrition of Adolescent Girls Research Program Report Series, no. 7. Washington, DC: International Center for Research on Women.

Bouis, Howarth E. et al. 1997. "Investing in adolescents in rural households: A Philippine case study," unpublished report presented to the International Food Policy Research Institute, Washington, DC.

Boyer, Debra and David Fine. 1992. "Sexual abuse as a factor in adolescent pregnancy and child maltreatment," *Family Planning Perspectives* 24, no. 1: 4–11, 19.

Brady, Martha. 1997. Personal communication.

———. 1998. "Laying the foundation for girls' healthy futures: Can sports play a role?" *Studies in Family Planning* 29, no. 1: 79–82.

Brody, Eugene B. 1981. *Sex, Contraception, and Motherhood in Jamaica*. Cambridge, MA: Harvard University Press.

Brown, Lynn R. and Lawrence Haddad. 1995. "Time allocation patterns and time burdens: A gendered analysis of seven countries," unpublished report prepared for the International Food Policy Research Institute, Washington, DC.

Brown, Sarah S. and Leon Eisenberg (eds.). 1995. *The Best Intentions: Unintended Pregnancy and the Well-Being of Children and Families*. Washington, DC: National Academy Press.

Bruce, Judith. 1976. "Women's organization: A resource for family planning and development," *Family Planning Perspectives* 8, no. 6: 291–297.

Bruce, Judith and Cynthia B. Lloyd. 1997. "Finding the ties that bind: Beyond headship and household," in Lawrence Haddad, John Hoddinott, and Harold Alderman (eds.), *Intrahousehold Resource Allocation in Developing Countries: Models, Methods, and Policy*. Baltimore: Johns Hopkins University Press, pp. 213–228.

Bruce, Judith, Cynthia B. Lloyd, and Ann Leonard. 1995. *Families in Focus: New Perspectives on Mothers, Fathers, and Children*. New York: Population Council.

Buckley, Thomas and Alma Gottlieb. 1988. "A critical appraisal of theories of menstrual symbolism," in Thomas Buckley and Alma Gottlieb (eds.), *Blood Magic: The Anthropology of Menstruation*. Berkeley: University of California Press, pp. 1–50.

Burra, Neera. 1997. *Born to Work: Child Labour in India*. Delhi: Oxford India Paperbacks.

Bustillo, Ines. 1993. "Latin America and the Caribbean," in Elizabeth M. King and M. Anne Hill (eds.), *Women's Education in Developing Countries: Barriers, Benefits, and Policies*. Baltimore: Johns Hopkins University Press, pp. 175–210.

Buvinic, Mayra. 1998. "The costs of adolescent childbearing: Evidence from Chile, Barbados, Guatemala, and Mexico," *Studies in Family Planning* 29, no. 2: 201–209.

Buvinic, Mayra and Kathleen Kurz. 1997. "Prospects for young mothers and their children: A review of the evidence on consequences of adolescent childbearing in developing countries," paper presented at the Workshop on Adolescent Sexuality and Reproductive Health in Developing Countries: Trends and Interventions, National Academy of Sciences, 25 March, Washington, DC.

Cain, Mead T. 1977. "The economic activities of children in a village in Bangladesh," *Population and Development Review 3*, no. 3: 201–227.

———. 1984. "Women's status and fertility in developing countries: Son preference and economic security," World Bank Staff Working Paper no. 682. Washington, DC.

Caldwell, John C., P. H. Reddy, and Pat Caldwell. 1983. "The causes of marriage change in South India," *Population Studies* 37, no. 3: 343–361.

————. 1985. "Educational transition in rural South India," *Population and Development Review* 11, no. 1: 29–51.

Caldwell, John C., Pat Caldwell, Bruce K. Caldwell, and Indrani Pieris. 1998. "The construction of adolescence in a changing world: Implications for sexuality, reproduction, and marriage," *Studies in Family Planning* 29, no. 2: 137–153.

Calvès, Anne-Emmanuèle, Gretchen T. Cornwell, and Parfait E. Enyegue. 1996. "Adolescent sexual activity in sub-Saharan Africa: Do men have the same strategies and motivations as women?" Population Research Institute Working Paper AD96-04. University Park: Population Research Institute, Pennsylvania State University.

Cameron, N. and I. Nagdee. 1996. "Menarcheal age in two generations of South African Indians," *Annals of Human Biology* 23, no. 2: 113–119.

Card, Josefina J. 1993. *Handbook of Adolescent Sexuality and Pregnancy: Research and Evaluation Instruments.* Newbury Park, CA: Sage Publications.

Casterline, John B., Aurora E. Perez, and Ann E. Biddlecom. 1997. "Factors underlying unmet need for family planning in the Philippines," *Studies in Family Planning* 28, no. 3: 173–191.

Cates, Willard, Jr. and Melissa McPheeters. 1997. "Adolescents and sexually transmitted diseases: Current risks and future consequences," paper presented at the Workshop on Adolescent Sexuality and Reproductive Health in Developing Countries: Trends and Interventions, National Academy of Sciences, 25 March, Washington, DC.

Center for Human Resource Research. 1994. *The National Longitudinal Surveys Handbook, 1994.* Columbus: Ohio State University.

Centers for Disease Control and Prevention (CDC). 1991. "Premarital sexual experience among adolescent women, United States, 1970–1988," *Morbidity and Mortality Weekly Report* 130, nos. 51/52: 929–932.

Centre for Mass Education in Science. 1993. *"Adolescent Girls' Program": A Program to Empower the Adolescent Girls from Rural Poor Families.* Dhaka.

Chakravarty, Kanta. 1994. "Age at menarche among the Rajbashi women of North Bengal," *Journal of the Assam Science Society* 36, no. 1: 49–52.

Chaney, Elsa and Mary Castro. 1989. *Muchachas No More: Household Workers in Latin America and the Caribbean.* Philadelphia: Temple University Press.

Chantrakar, Sompop. 1994. "Programme for girls in especially difficult circumstances: A case study of Thailand: Daughters' education programme," paper presented at the UNICEF Interregional Consultation on the Girl Child, 10–16 February, Anand, India.

Coale, Ansley J. and Paul Demeny. 1983. *Regional Model Life Tables and Stable Populations.* Second Edition. New York: Academic Press.

Commonwealth Secretariat. 1990. "Approaching youth policy: Considerations for national youth development policy," Policy Document no. 1. London.

Cooper, Diana E., John M. Paxman, and Rahema Mwateba. 1988. *Confronting Schoolgirl Pregnancy in Tanzania: An Interim Evaluation of the Dar-es-Salaam Youth Vocational Centre Adolescent Drop-Out Program.* Boston: The Pathfinder Fund.

Cotton, Ann. 1996. *Supporting the Education of Girls in Sub-Saharan Africa.* Cambridge, UK: Cambridge Female Education Trust.

———. 1997. *The CamFed Programme: Educating Girls in Sub-Saharan Africa.* Cambridge, UK: Cambridge Female Education Trust.

D'Amico, R. and N. L. Maxwell. 1992. "The impact of post-school joblessness on male black–white wage differentials," *Industrial Relations* 33, no. 2: 184–205.

Daley, Suzanne. 1998. "Young, vulnerable, and violated in the new South Africa," *The New York Times Magazine* 12 July: 30–33.

Das Gupta, Monica. 1996. "Life course perspectives on women's autonomy and health outcomes," *Health Transition Review* 6 (Supp.): 213–231.

Demeny, Paul. 1988. "Social science and population policy," *Population and Development Review* 14, no. 3: 451–479.

Devasia, Leelamma and V. V. Devasia. 1991. *Girl Child in India.* New Delhi: Ashish Publishing House.

Dixon, Ruth B. 1978. *Rural Women at Work: Strategies for Development in South Asia.* Baltimore: Johns Hopkins University Press.

Dixon-Mueller, Ruth B. 1985. *Women's Work in Third World Agriculture: Concepts and Indicators.* Geneva: International Labour Office.

Dryfoos, Joy G. 1990. *Adolescents at Risk: Prevalence and Prevention.* New York: Oxford University Press.

El-Tawila, Sahar et al. 1998. "Adolescence and social change: Health status, educational achievement, economic roles and socialization of adolescents in Egypt," draft report. Cairo: Population Council.

El-Zanaty, Fatma et al. 1996. *Egypt Demographic and Health Survey, 1995.* Calverton, MD: National Population Council, Egypt and Macro International.

Engle, Patrice L. and Craig Loftin. 1997. "Improving child growth and development through investments in fathering in urban and rural Nicaragua," proposal submitted to the Population Council's Gender, Family, and Development Program.

Engle, Patrice L. and Robert K. Smidt. 1996. "Influences of adolescent childbearing and marital status at first birth on rural Guatemalan women and children," Working Paper Series on Family Structure, Female Headship, and Maintenance of Families and Poverty. New York: Population Council and the International Center for Research on Women.

Erulkar, Annabel S. and Barbara S. Mensch. 1997a. "Gender differences in the dating experiences and sexual behavior of adolescents in Kenya," paper presented at the 23rd General Conference of the International Union for the Scientific Study of Population, Beijing.

———. 1997b. *Evaluation of the Youth Centre Programme of the Family Planning Association of Kenya.* Nairobi: Population Council and the Family Planning Association of Kenya.

Esty, Daniel C. et al. 1995. *State Failure Task Force Report.* Langley, VA: Central Intelligence Agency.

Ezeh, Alex C., Michka Seroussi, and Hendrik Raggers. 1996. "Men's fertility, contraceptive use, and reproductive preferences," *DHS Comparative Studies*, no. 18. Calverton, MD: Macro International Inc.

Faiz, Ladly, Hasina Banu, and Devi Sharma. 1996. *Adolescent Family Life Education: Review of Curriculum.* Dhaka: Population Research and Development

Associates and Population Council Asia and Near East Operations Research and Technical Assistance Project.

Ferguson, Alan. 1988. *Schoolgirl Pregnancy in Kenya: Report of a Study of Discontinuation Rates and Associated Factors*. Nairobi: Division of Family Health, Kenyan Ministry of Health.

Ferguson, Jane. 1996. "Adolescent health and development, family, and reproductive health: World Health Organization view of policy in adolescent health service and program development," mimeographed, 30 April.

Feyisetan, Bamikale and Anne R. Pebley. 1989. "Premarital sexuality in urban Nigeria," *Studies in Family Planning* 20, no. 6: 343–354.

Furstenberg, Frank F., Jr. 1976. "The social consequences of teenage parenthood," *Family Planning Perspectives* 8, no. 4: 148–167.

———. 1998. "When will teenage childbearing become a problem? The implications of Western experience for developing countries," *Studies in Family Planning* 29, no. 2: 246–253.

Furstenberg, Frank F., Jr., J. Brooks-Gunn, and S. Philip Morgan. 1987. *Adolescent Mothers in Later Life*. New York: Cambridge University Press.

Geronimus, Arline T. and Sanders Korenman. 1992. "The socio-economic consequences of teen childbearing reconsidered," *The Quarterly Journal of Economics* 107, no. 4: 1187–1215.

Geronimus, Arline T., Sanders Korenman, and Marianne M. Hillemeier. 1994. "Does young maternal age adversely affect child development? Evidence from cousin comparisons in the United States," *Population and Development Review* 20, no. 3: 585–609.

Gill, Andrew M. and Robert J. Michaels. 1992. "Does drug use lower wages?" *Industrial and Labor Relations Review* 45, no. 3: 419–434.

Görgen, Regina, Mohamed L. Yansané, Michael Marx, and Dominque Millimounou. 1998. "Sexual behavior and attitudes among unmarried urban youths in Guinea," *International Family Planning Perspectives* 24, no. 2: 65–71.

Government of Malawi. 1995. *Government of Malawi Youth Strategy*. Lilongwe.

Greene, Margaret E. 1997. "Watering the neighbour's garden: Investing in adolescent girls in India," South and East Asia Regional Working Paper no. 7. New Delhi: Population Council.

Greenhalgh, Susan. 1996. "The social construction of population science: An intellectual, institutional, and political history of twentieth-century demography," *Comparative Studies of Society and History* 38, no. 1: 26–66.

Grogger, Jeff. 1992. "Arrests, persistent youth joblessness, and black/white employment differentials," *The Review of Economics and Statistics* 64, no. 1: 100–106.

Haider, Syed Jahangeer, Shamsun Nehar Saleh, Nahid Kamal, and Alan Gray. 1997. *Study of Adolescents: Dynamics of Perception, Attitude, Knowledge and Use of Reproductive Health Care*. Dhaka: Population Council.

Harlow, Sioban D. 1995. *What We Do Know and Do Not Know About the Menstrual Cycle; or, Questions Scientists Could Be Asking*. New York: Population Council, Robert H. Ebert Program on Critical Issues in Reproductive Health.

Haurin, R. Jean. 1992. "Patterns of childhood residence and the relationship to young adult outcomes," *Journal of Marriage and the Family* 54, no. 4: 846–860.

Hayes, Cheryl D. (ed.). 1987. *Risking the Future: Adolescent Sexuality, Pregnancy, and Childbearing*, Vol. 1. Washington, DC: National Academy Press for the National Research Council.

Herdt, Gilbert H. (ed.). 1982. *Rituals of Manhood: Male Initiation in Papua New Guinea*. Berkeley: University of California Press.

Herrera, Linda. 1992. "Scenes of schooling: Inside a girls' school in Cairo," Cairo Papers in Social Science, Vol. 15, monograph 1. Cairo: American University in Cairo Press.

Herz, Barbara K. and Shahidur Khandker. 1991. "Women's work: Education and family welfare in Peru," World Bank Discussion Paper no. 116. Washington, DC.

Herz, Barbara et al. 1991. "Letting girls learn: Promising approaches in primary and secondary education," World Bank Discussion Paper no. 133. Washington, DC.

Hill, M. Anne and Elizabeth M. King. 1993. "Women's education in developing countries: An overview," in Elizabeth M. King and M. Anne Hill (eds.), *Women's Education in Developing Countries: Barriers, Benefits, and Policies*. Baltimore: Johns Hopkins University Press, pp. 1–50.

Hirsch, Jennifer S. and Gary Barker. 1992. *Adolescents and Unsafe Abortion in Developing Countries: A Preventable Tragedy*. Washington, DC: Center for Population Options.

Hoffman, Saul D., Michael Foster, and Frank F. Furstenberg, Jr. 1993. "Re-evaluating the costs of teenage childbearing," *Demography* 30, no. 1: 1–13.

Hughes, Jane and Ann P. McCauley. 1998. "Improving the fit: Adolescents' needs and future programs for sexual and reproductive health in developing countries," *Studies in Family Planning* 29, no. 2: 233–245.

Huntington, Dale, Cheryl Lettenmaier, and Isaac Obeng-Quaidoo. 1990. "User's perspective of counseling training in Ghana: The 'mystery client' trial," *Studies in Family Planning* 21, no. 3: 171–177.

Hussain, Mahbub. 1986. "Credit for alleviation of rural poverty: The experience of Grameen Bank in Bangladesh," Dhaka: Agriculture and Rural Development Division, Bangladesh Institute of Development Studies. Mimeograph.

Huygens, Pierre, Ellen Kajura, Janet Seeley, and Tom Barton. 1996. "Rethinking methods for the study of sexual behaviour," *Social Science and Medicine* 42, no. 2: 221–231.

Ibrahim Barbara, Barbara S. Mensch, and Omaima El Gibaly. 1998. "Transitions to manhood: Socialization to gender roles and marriage among Egyptian adolescent boys," paper presented at the International Union for the Scientific Study of Population Seminar on Men, Family Formation, and Reproduction, 13–15 May, Buenos Aires.

Ibrahim, Saad Eddin. 1995. "State, women, and civil society: An evaluation of Egypt's population policy," in Carla Makhlouf Obermeyer (ed.), *Family, Gender, and Population in the Middle East: Policies in Context*. Cairo: American University in Cairo Press, pp. 57–79.

International Center for Research on Women (ICRW). 1997. "Researching women: A research program on unmet need for family planning," *ICRW Information Bulletin*, January. Washington, DC.

International Labour Office (ILO). 1996. *Yearbook of Labour Statistics*. Geneva.

International Youth Foundation. 1992. *A Global Exchange of Effective Programs Serving Children and Youth, Volume 1: Educational Centre for Adolescent Women/Peer Counselling by Teens*. Gaborone, Botswana.

Jabbar, Fahad and Simin S. Wong. 1988. "Age at menarche and reproductive pattern among Saudi women," *Journal of the Royal Society of Health* 108, no. 3: 94–96.

Jain, Shobhita. 1988. *Sexual Equality: Workers in an Asian Plantation System*. New Delhi: Sterling Publishers.

Jaruratanasirikul, S. and L. Lebel. 1995. "Ages at thelarche and menarche: Study in southern Thai schoolgirls," *Journal of the Medical Association of Thailand* 78, no. 10: 517–520.

Jeffery, Patricia and Roger Jeffery. 1996. "What's the benefit of being educated? Girls' schooling, women's autonomy, and fertility outcomes in Bijnor," in Roger Jeffery and Alaka M. Basu (eds.), *Girls' Schooling, Women's Autonomy and Fertility Change in South Asia*. New Delhi: Sage Publications, pp. 150–183.

Jejeebhoy, Shireen J. 1995. *Women's Education, Autonomy, and Reproductive Behaviour: Experience from Developing Countries*. Oxford: Clarendon Press.

———. 1996. "Adolescent sexual and reproductive behavior: A review of the evidence from India," ICRW Working Paper no. 3. Washington, DC.

Jiggins, Janice. 1997. Personal communication.

Johnston, Heidi Bart and Kenneth H. Hill. 1996. "Induced abortion in the developing world: Indirect estimates," *International Family Planning Perspectives* 22, no. 3: 108–134, 137.

Jones, Elise F. et al. 1989. *Teenage Pregnancy in Industrialized Countries*. New Haven: Yale University Press.

Kaestner, Robert. 1991. "The effect of illicit drug use on the wages of young adults," *Journal of Labor Economics* 9, no. 4: 381–412.

Kakar, Sudhir. 1981. *The Inner World: A Psychoanalytic Study of Childhood and Society in India*. New Delhi: Oxford University Press.

Kanhere, Usha S. 1989. "Different socialization of boys and girls: A study of lower socioeconomic households among Gujarati caste/communities in Ahmedabad," in Maithreyi Krishnaraj and Karuna Chanana (eds.), *Gender and the Household Domain: Social and Cultural Dimensions*. New Delhi: Sage Publications, pp. 31–54.

Kennedy, Paul M. 1993. *Preparing for the Twenty-First Century*. New York: Vintage Books.

Kett, Joseph F. 1971. "Adolescence and youth in nineteenth-century America," in Theodore K. Rabb and Robert I. Rotberg (eds.), *The Family in History: Interdisciplinary Essays*. New York: Harper & Row.

Khan, Shahrukh R. 1993. "South Asia," in Elizabeth M. King and M. Anne Hill (eds.), *Women's Education in Developing Countries: Barriers, Benefits, and Policies*. Baltimore: Johns Hopkins University Press, pp. 211–246.

Khattab, Hind. 1996. "Women's perceptions of sexuality in rural Giza," Monograph in Reproductive Health No. 1. Cairo: Population Council Reproductive Health Working Group.

Kiem, Christian G. 1993. *Growing Up in Indonesia: Youth and Social Change in a Moluccan Town*. Saarbrücken, Germany; Fort Lauderdale, FL: Breitenbach.

Kiragu, Karungari and Laurie S. Zabin. 1993. "The correlates of premarital sexual activity among school-age adolescents in Kenya," *International Family Planning Perspectives* 19, no. 3: 92–97, 109.

Klerman, Jacob A. and Lynn Karoly. 1994. "Young men and the transition to stable employment," *Monthly Labor Review* 117, no. 8: 31–48.

Knodel, John and Gavin W. Jones. 1996. "Post-Cairo population policy: Does promoting girls' schooling miss the mark?" *Population and Development Review* 22, no. 4: 683–702.

Kuper, Adam. 1982. *Wives for Cattle: Bridewealth and Marriage in Southern Africa*. London: Routledge and Kegan Paul.

Kurz, Kathleen M. and Charlotte Johnson-Welch. 1994. *The Nutrition and Lives of Adolescents in Developing Countries: Findings from the Nutrition of Adolescent Girls Research Program*. Washington, DC: ICRW.

Laumann, Edward O. 1996. *Early Sexual Experiences: How Voluntary? How Violent?* Sexuality and American Social Policy Seminar Series. Menlo Park, CA: Henry J. Kaiser Family Foundation.

LeVine, Robert A. 1982. "Influences of women's schooling on maternal behavior in the third world," in Gail P. Kelly and Carolyn M. Elliott (eds.), *Women's Education in the Third World: Comparative Perspectives*. Albany, NY: State University of New York Press, pp. 283–310.

LeVine, Robert A. et al. 1994. *Childcare and Culture: Lessons from Africa*. New York: Cambridge University Press.

Levine, Sarah E. 1993. *Dolor y Alegría: Women and Social Change in Urban Mexico*. Madison: University of Wisconsin Press.

Levison, Deborah and Karin S. Moe. 1997. "Household work as a deterrent to schooling: An analysis of adolescent girls in Peru," paper presented at the Annual Meeting of the Population Association of America, 27–29 March, Washington, DC.

Lloyd, Cynthia B. 1991. "The contribution of the World Fertility Surveys to an understanding of the relationship between women's work and fertility," *Studies in Family Planning* 22, no. 3: 144–161.

Lloyd, Cynthia B. and Ann K. Blanc. 1996. "Children's schooling in sub-Saharan Africa: The role of fathers, mothers, and others," *Population and Development Review* 22, no. 2: 265–298.

Lloyd, Cynthia B. and Sonalde Desai. 1992. "Children's living arrangements in developing countries," *Population Research and Policy Review* 11, no. 3: 193–216.

Lloyd, Cynthia B. and Anastasia J. Gage. 1995. "High fertility and the intergenerational transmission of gender inequality: Children's transition to adulthood in Ghana," in Paulina Makinwa and An-Magritt Jensen (eds.), *Women's Position and Demographic Change in Sub-Saharan Africa*. Liège, Belgium: International Union for the Scientific Study of Population, pp. 127–146.

Lloyd, Cynthia B., Carol Kaufman, and Paul Hewett. 1998. "Education transitions in sub-Saharan Africa: Implications for fertility change," paper presented at the International Union for the Scientific Study of Population Seminar on Reproductive Change in Sub-Saharan Africa, 2–4 November, Nairobi.

Lloyd, Cynthia B., Barbara S. Mensch, and Wesley Clark. 1998. "The effects of primary school quality on the educational participation and attainment of Kenyan girls and boys," paper presented at the Annual Meeting of the Population Association of America, 2-4 April, Chicago.

Loffredo, Sasha et al. 1994. *World Youth 1994: Special Focus on Reproductive Health Wall Chart*. Washington, DC: Population Reference Bureau and Center for Population Options.

Luker, Kristin. 1996. *Dubious Conceptions: The Politics of Teenage Pregnancy*. Cambridge, MA: Harvard University Press.

Macro International. 1997. *DHS Newsletter* 9, no. 1.

Maher, Vanessa. 1974. *Women and Property in Morocco: Their Changing Relation to the Process of Social Stratification in the Middle Atlas*. New York: Cambridge University Press.

Males, Mike and Kenneth S. Y. Chew. 1996. "The ages of fathers in California adolescent births, 1993," *American Journal of Public Health* 86, no. 4: 565–567.

Mandelbaum, David G. 1988. *Women's Seclusion and Men's Honor: Sex Roles in North India, Bangladesh, and Pakistan*. Tucson: University of Arizona Press.

Manning, Wendy D. and Pamela Smock. 1995. "Why marry? Race and the transition to marriage among cohabitors," *Demography* 32, no. 4: 509–520.

Marques, Magaly. 1993. "Gente Joven/Young People: A dialogue on sexuality with adolescents in Mexico," *Quality/Calidad/Qualité*, no. 5. New York: Population Council.

Mathare Youth Sports Association (MYSA). 1996. Brochure. Nairobi, Kenya.

Mathews, Jessica T. 1997. "Power shift," *Foreign Affairs* 76, no. 1: 50–66.

McCauley, Ann P. and Cynthia Salter. 1995. "Meeting the Needs of Young Adults," *Population Reports,* series J, no. 41: 1–43.

McDevitt, Thomas M. et al. 1996. *Trends in Adolescent Fertility and Contraceptive Use in the Developing World*. Washington, DC: U.S. Bureau of the Census.

McNeil, Pamela, Freya Olafson, Dorian L. Powell, and Jean Jackson. 1983. "The Women's Centre in Jamaica: An innovative project for adolescent mothers," *Studies in Family Planning* 14, no. 5: 143–149.

Meekers, Dominique. 1992. "The process of marriage in African societies: A multiple indicator approach," *Population and Development Review* 18, no. 1: 61–78.

Meekers, Dominique and Ghyasuddin Ahmed. 1997. "Pregnancy-related school dropouts in Botswana," PSI Research Division Working Paper no. 1. Washington, DC: Population Services International.

Meekers, Dominique, Anastasia Gage, and Li Zhan. 1995. "Preparing adolescents for adulthood: Family life education and pregnancy-related school expulsion in Kenya," *Population Research and Policy Review* 14: 91–110.

Mensch, Barbara S. and Denise B. Kandel. 1988. "Dropping out of high school and drug involvement," *Sociology of Education* 61: 95–113.

Mensch, Barbara S. and Cynthia B. Lloyd. 1998. "Gender differences in the schooling experiences of adolescents in low-income countries: The case of Kenya," *Studies in Family Planning* 29, no. 2: 167–184.

Michael, R. T. and N. B. Tuma. 1984. "Youth employment: Does life begin at 16?" *Journal of Labor Economics* 2, no. 4: 464–476.

Miller, Barbara D. 1981. *The Endangered Sex: Neglect of Female Children in Rural North India.* Ithaca: Cornell University Press.

Minge-Klevana, Wanda. 1980. "Does labor time decrease with industrialization? A survey of time-allocation studies," *Current Anthropology* 21, no. 3: 279–298.

Misra, Arunditi. 1995. "Menstruation: Crisis in adolescence," in Sunil Mehra (ed.), *Adolescent Girl: An Indian Perspective.* New Delhi: MAMTA, pp. 75–78.

Molzan-Turan, Janet. 1996. *Postpartum Family Planning and Health in Istanbul: Bringing Fathers into the Picture.* Istanbul: Istanbul University, Institute of Child Health.

———. 1997. Personal communication.

Moore, Kristin A. et al. 1987. "Statistical appendix: Trends in adolescent sexual and fertility behavior," in Sandra L. Hofferth and Cheryl D. Hayes (eds.), *Risking the Future: Adolescent Sexuality, Pregnancy, and Childbearing,* Vol. II. Washington, DC: National Academy Press, pp. 353–520.

Morris, Leo. 1992. "Sexual experience and use of contraception among young adults in Latin America," in Centers for Disease Control, Special Focus II: Public Health Surveillance and International Health, *CDC Surveillance Summaries* 41, no. SS-4: 27–40.

———. 1994. "Sexual behavior of young adults in Latin America," *Advances in Population* 2: 231–252.

———. 1996. Personal communication.

Morris, Leo, Charles W. Warren, and Sevgi O. Aral. 1993. "Measuring adolescent sexual behaviors and related health outcomes," *Public Health Reports* 108, Supplement 1: 31–36.

Mortimer, Jeylan T., Michael D. Finch, Timothy J. Owens, and Michael Shanahan. 1990. "Gender and work in adolescence," *Youth and Society* 22, no. 2: 201–224.

Mosher, William D. 1998. "Design and operation of the 1995 National Survey of Family Growth," *Family Planning Perspectives* 30, no. 1: 43–46.

Naré, Christine, Karen Katz, and Elizabeth Tolley. 1996. *Measuring Access to Family Planning Education and Services for Young Adults in Dakar, Senegal.* Research Triangle Park, NC: Family Health International.

Nathanson, Constance A. 1991. *Dangerous Passage: The Social Control of Sexuality in Women's Adolescence.* Philadelphia: Temple University Press.

National Center for Health Statistics, U.S. Department of Health and Human Services. 1995. *Report to Congress on Out-of-Wedlock Childbearing,* DHHS Pub. no. (PHS) 95-1257. Hyattsville, MD: National Center for Health Statistics.

National Statistics Office of Eritrea and Macro International. 1997. *Eritrea Demographic and Health Survey, 1995.* Calverton, MD.

Nawar, Laila, Cynthia B. Lloyd, and Barbara Ibrahim. 1995. "Women's autonomy and gender roles in Egyptian families," in Carla Makhlouf Obermeyer (ed.), *Family, Gender, and Population in the Middle East: Policies in Context*. Cairo: American University in Cairo Press, pp. 147–178.

Netherlands Ministry of Foreign Affairs and Netherlands Ministry of Health, Welfare, and Sport. 1998. "Sport in development: Teamwork scores!" Policy memorandum on sport in the context of development cooperation. The Hague.

Nichols, Douglas, O. A. Ladipo, John M. Paxman, and E. O. Otolorin. 1986. "Sexual behavior, contraceptive practice, and reproductive health among Nigerian adolescents," *Studies in Family Planning* 17, no. 2: 100–106.

Nichols, Douglas, Emile T. Woods, Deborah S. Gates, and Joyce Sherman. 1987. "Sexual behavior, contraceptive practice, and reproductive health among Liberian adolescents," *Studies in Family Planning* 18, no. 3: 169–176.

Noble, Jeanne, Jane Cover, and Machuko Yanagishita. 1996. "The world's youth, 1996," Population Reference Bureau datasheet. Washington, DC: Population Reference Bureau.

Nock, Steven L. 1998. "The consequences of premarital fatherhood," *American Sociological Review* 63, no. 2: 250–263.

Nunn, Andrew J. et al. 1994. "Risk factors of HIV-1 infection in adults in a rural Ugandan community: A population study," *AIDS* 8, no. 1: 81–86.

Odaga, Adhiambo and Ward Heneveld. 1995. "Girls and schools in sub-Saharan Africa: From analysis to action," World Bank Technical Paper no. 298. Washington, DC.

Oppong, Christine. 1995. *A High Price to Pay: For Education, Subsistence, or a Place in the Job Market*. Canberra: Australian National University, National Centre for Epidemiology and Population Health.

Ortiz, V. and R. Santana Cooney. 1984. "Sex-role attitudes and labor force participation among young Hispanic females and non-Hispanic white females," *Social Science Quarterly* 65, no. 2: 392–400.

Orubuloye, Israel Olantuji, John C. Caldwell, Pat Caldwell, and Gigi Santow. 1994. "Sexual Networking and AIDS in Sub-Saharan Africa," *Health Transition Series* no. 4. Canberra: Australian National University Health Transition Centre.

Osom, John. 1989. *Moral Implication of High Bride-Price in Nigeria: Annany [i.e. Annang] Case Survey*. Rome: Pontificia Universitas Lateranensis, Institutum Superius Theologiae Moralis.

Oucho, John O. and William T. S. Gould. 1993. "Internal migration, urbanization, and population distribution," in Karen A. Foote, Kenneth H. Hill, and Linda G. Martin (eds.), *Demographic Change in Sub-Saharan Africa*. Washington, DC: National Academy Press, pp. 256–296.

Pantelides, Edith Alejandra, Rosa N. Geldstein, and Graciela Infesta Dominguez. 1995. *Imágenes de Género y Conducta Reproductiva en la Adolescencia*. Buenos Aires: Centro de Estudios de Población (CENEP).

Papanek, Hanna. 1982. "Purdah: Separate worlds and symbolic shelter," in Hanna Papanek and G. Minault (eds.), *Separate Worlds*. Delhi: Chanakya Publications, pp. 3–53.

Peplinsky, Nancy. 1994. *Addressing Needs and Opportunities: A Survey of Programs for Adolescents*. Washington, DC: International Center for Research on Women.

Phillips, A. S. 1973. *Adolescence in Jamaica*. London: Jamaica Publishing House, Macmillan.

Phiri, Alford and Annabel S. Erulkar. 1997. *A Situation Analysis of the Zimbabwe National Family Planning Council's Youth Centres: Baseline Assessment*. Nairobi: Zimbabwe National Family Planning Council and Population Council.

Population and Community Development Association. 1995. "AIDS education and alternatives to prostitution in northern Thailand," unpublished project document. Bangkok.

Population Council. 1996. "Innovative programmatic approaches toward working with adolescent girls," unpublished report compiled for the "Take Back Young Lives" seminar at The World Bank, 30 April, Washington, DC.

Population Council and Overseas Development Council. 1998. *What Can Be Done to Foster Multisectoral Population Policies? Summary Report of a Seminar*. New York: Population Council and Overseas Development Council.

Population Reference Bureau. 1997. "1997 World Population Data Sheet," Washington, DC.

Powers, Daniel A. 1994. "Transitions into idleness among white, black, and Hispanic youth: Some determinants and policy implications of weak labor force attachment," *Sociological Perspectives* 37, no. 2: 183–201.

Presser, Harriet. 1971. "The timing at first birth: Female roles and black fertility," *Milbank Memorial Fund Quarterly* 49: 329–391.

Pyne, H. H. 1992. *AIDS and Prostitution in Thailand: Case Study of Burmese Prostitutes in Ranong*. Boston: Massachusetts Institute of Technology.

Rajaretnam, T. and R. V. Deshpande. 1994. "Factors inhibiting the use of reversible contraceptive methods in rural south India," *Studies in Family Planning* 25, no. 2: 111–121.

Resnick, Michael D. et al. 1997. "Protecting adolescents from harm: Findings from the National Longitudinal Study on Adolescent Health," *Journal of the American Medical Association* 278, no. 10: 823–832.

Romero, Patricia W. (ed.). 1988. *Life Histories of African Women*. Atlantic Highlands, NJ: Ashfield Press.

Russell-Brown, Pauline, Patrice L. Engle, and John W. Townsend. 1992. "The effects of early childbearing on women's status in Barbados," Working Paper Series on Family Structure, Female Headship, and Maintenance of Families and Poverty. New York: Population Council and the International Center for Research on Women.

Rutstein, Shea O. and George T. Bicego. 1990. "Assessment of the quality of data used to ascertain eligibility and age in the Demographic and Health Surveys," in Institute for Resource Development, *An Assessment of DHS-1 Data Quality*. DHS Methodological Reports no. 1. Columbia, MD: Institute for Resource Development/Macro Systems.

Sanday, Peggy R. 1974. "Female status in the public domain," in Michelle Rosaldo and Louise Lamphere (eds.), *Women, Culture, and Society*. Stanford, CA: Stanford University Press, pp. 189–206.

Sandefur, Gary D., Sara S. McLanahan, and Roger A. Wojtkiewicz. 1992. "The effects of parental marital status during adolescence on high school graduation," *Social Forces* 71, no. 1: 103–121.

Sathar, Zeba A. 1998. Personal communication.

Sathar, Zeba A. and Cynthia B. Lloyd. 1994. "Who gets primary schooling in Pakistan: Inequalities among and within families," *Pakistan Development Review* 33, no. 2: 103–134.

Schlegel, Alice. 1995. "A cross-cultural approach to adolescence," *Ethos* 23, no. 1: 15–32.

Schultz, T. Paul. 1993. "Returns to women's education," in Elizabeth M. King and M. Anne Hill (eds.), *Women's Education in Developing Countries: Barriers, Benefits, and Policies.* Baltimore: Johns Hopkins University Press, pp. 51–99.

Sebstad, Jennefer. 1991. "Gender and employment in Kenya: Analysis of the 1988 rural and 1986 urban labour force surveys," unpublished report presented to the Government of Kenya's Ministry of Planning and National Development, Long Range Planning Project.

Sen, Amartya. 1997. "Editorial: Human capital and human capability," *World Development* 25, no. 12: 1959–1961.

Senderowitz, Judith. 1995. "Adolescent health: Reassessing the passage to adulthood," World Bank Discussion Paper no. 272. Washington, DC.

Sharma, Neelam and A. B. Hiramani. 1985. "Estimation of reproductive span of Brahmin and Chaudhary females of Kangra (Himachal Pradesh)," *Journal of Family Welfare* 32, no. 1: 25–29.

Shweder, Richard A. 1995. Personal communication.

Singh, Susheela. 1998a. Personal communication.

———. 1998b. "Adolescent childbearing in developing countries: A global review," *Studies in Family Planning* 29, no. 2: 117–136.

Singh, Susheela and Stanley Henshaw. 1996. "The incidence of abortion: A worldwide overview focusing on methodology and on Latin America," paper presented at the IUSSP Seminar on Socio-Cultural and Political Aspects of Abortion from an Anthropological Perspective, 25–28 March, Trivandrum, India.

Singh, Susheela and Renee Samara. 1996. "Early marriage among women in developing countries," *International Family Planning Perspectives* 22, no. 4: 148–157, 175.

Singh, Susheela and Deirdre Wulf. 1990. *Today's Adolescents, Tomorrow's Parents: A Portrait of the Americas.* New York: Alan Guttmacher Institute.

———. 1993. "The likelihood of induced abortion among women hospitalized for abortion complications in four Latin American countries," *International Family Planning Perspectives* 19, no. 4: 134–141.

———. 1994. "Estimated levels of induced abortion in six Latin American countries," *International Family Planning Perspectives* 20, no. 1: 4–13.

Sohoni, Neera Kuckreja. 1995. *The Burden of Girlhood.* Oakland, CA: Third Party Publishing Company.

Standing, Guy. 1989. "Global feminization through flexible labor," *World Development* 17, no. 7: 1077–1095.

Stewart, Lindsay et al. 1996. "Consequences of sexual abuse of adolescents," *Reproductive Health Matters* no. 7: 129–134.

Subbarao, K. and Laura Raney. 1993. "Social gains from female education: A cross-national study," World Bank Discussion Paper no. 194. Washington, DC.

Summers, Lawrence H. 1992. "Essay: The most influential investment," *Scientific American* 267, no. 2: 132.

Sweet, James A. and Larry L. Bumpass. 1990. "Young adults' views of marriage, cohabitation, and family," NSFH Working Paper no. 33. Madison: Center for Demography and Ecology, University of Wisconsin.

Tenorio Ambrosi, Rodrigo, María Soledad Farrín, and Paul Bonilla. 1995. *La Cultura Sexual de los Adolescentes*. Quito: Ediciones Abya-Yala.

Twa-Twa, Jeremiahs M. 1997. "The role of the environment in the sexual activity of school students in Tororo and Pallisa districts of Uganda," *Health Transition Review* 7 (Supp.): 67–81.

Ullrich, Helen E. 1977. "Caste differences between Brahmin and non-Brahmin women in a south Indian village," in Alice Schlegel (ed.), *Sexual Stratification: A Cross-Cultural View*. New York: Columbia University Press, pp. 94–108.

United Nations. 1995. *The World's Women: Trends and Statistics*. New York.

———. 1997. *The Sex and Age Distribution of the World Populations: The 1996 Revisions*. New York.

UNICEF. 1997. *The State of the World's Children 1997*. New York: Oxford University Press.

UNICEF Division of Communication. 1997. "Status of the Convention on the Rights of the Child," unpublished list, UNICEF, New York.

United Nations Educational, Scientific, and Cultural Organization (UNESCO). 1997. *Statistical Yearbook, 1996*. Paris and Lanham, MD: UNESCO Publishing and Bernan Press.

Veum, Jonathan R. and Andrea B. Weiss. 1993. "Education and the work histories of young adults," *Monthly Labor Review* 116, no. 4: 11–20.

Warren, Charles W. et al. 1998. "Sexual behavior among U.S. high school students, 1990–1995," *Family Planning Perspectives* 30, no. 4: 170–176.

Wasserheit, Judith et al. 1989. "Reprodutive tract infections in a family planning population in rural Bangladesh," *Studies in Family Planning* 20, no. 2: 69–80.

Wasserheit, Judith N. and King K. Holmes. 1992. "Reproductive tract infections: Challenges for international health policy, programs, and research," in Adrienne Germain, King K. Holmes, Peter Piot, and Judith N. Wasserheit (eds.), *Reproductive Tract Infections: Global Impact and Priorities for Women's Reproductive Health*. New York: Plenum Press.

Westoff, Charles F. and Akinrinola Bankole. 1995. "Unmet need: 1990–1994," *DHS Comparative Studies* no. 16. Calverton, MD: Macro International.

Westoff, Charles F., Ann K. Blanc, and Laura Nyblade. 1994. "Marriage and entry into parenthood," *DHS Comparative Studies* no. 10. Calverton, MD: Macro International.

Whiting Beatrice B. and John W. M. Whiting. 1990. "Preindustrial world, adolescence in," in Richard M. Lerner, Jeanne Brooks-Gunn, and Anne C. Petersen (eds.), *Encyclopedia of Adolescence*, Vol. II. New York: Garland, pp. 814–828.

Whiting, John W. M., Victoria Burbank, and Mitchell S. Ratner. 1986. "The duration of maidenhood across cultures," in Jane B. Lancaster and Beatrix A.

Hamburg (eds.), *School-Age Pregnancy and Parenthood: Biosocial Dimensions*. New York: Aldine de Gruyter, pp. 273–302.

Wilkinson, Marilyn I., Wamucii Njogu, and Noureddine Abderrahim. 1993. "The availability of family planning and maternal and child health services," *DHS Comparative Studies* no. 7. Columbia, MD: Macro International.

Williams, Judith R. 1968. *The Youth of Haouch et Harimi, A Lebanese Village*. Cambridge, MA: Harvard University Press.

Wolf, Diane L. 1992. *Factory Daughters: Gender, Household Dynamics, and Rural Industrialization in Java*. Berkeley: University of California Press.

Wolpin, Kenneth I. 1992. "The determinants of black–white differences in early employment careers: Search, layoffs, quits and endogenous wage growth," *Journal of Political Economy* 100, no. 3: 535–560.

Wojtkiewicz, Roger A. 1993. "Simplicity and complexity in the effects of parental structure on high school graduation," *Demography* 30, no. 4: 701–717.

World Health Organization (WHO). 1993. *The Health of Young People: A Challenge and a Promise*. Geneva.

WHO and UNICEF. 1995. *A Picture of Health? A Review and Annotated Bibliography of the Health of Young People in Developing Countries*. Geneva: WHO.

Xenos, Peter. 1997. "Survey sheds new light on marriage and sexuality in the Philippines," *Asia-Pacific Population and Policy* no. 42. Honolulu: East-West Center Program on Population.

Youri, Pat (ed.). 1994. *Female Adolescent Health and Sexuality in Kenyan Secondary Schools: A Survey Report*. Nairobi: African Medical and Research Foundation.

Zelnik, Melvin, John F. Kantner, and Kathleen Ford. 1981. *Sex and Pregnancy in Adolescence*. Beverly Hills, CA: Sage Publications.

Authors

Barbara S. Mensch is a Senior Associate in the Policy Research Division of the Population Council, New York.

Judith Bruce is Program Director for Gender, Family, and Development and a Senior Associate in the International Programs Division of the Population Council, New York.

Margaret E. Greene is a Senior Program Associate in the Center for Health and Gender Equity, Takoma Park, Maryland.